PRAYING FOR ETERNAL VICTORIES

# COACHING WITH A PURPOSE

A coach's playbook on walking an uncommon road of leading players to the feet of Jesus

## HEATHER HODGES

**BREAKTHROUGH**
CHRISTIAN PUBLISHING

Breakthrough Christian Publishing
PO Box 1011, Ketchum, OK 74349
www.breakthroughchristianpublishing.com

Published 2024
Printed in the United States of America

30 29 28 27 26 25 24    1 2 3 4 5

ISBN: 979-8-9907557-2-7

Copyright Case Number: 1-14082604084

# CONTENTS

# INTRODUCTION

Our road into coaching started after I sent my husband back to the altar for a third time to pray over "answering" the call from the Lord. We met when I was a student athletic trainer, and he was a baseball player for our college team. He came into the training room to ice his arm and kept coming back every day afterwards. He planned to be a physical therapist. In fact, he had already sent off graduate school applications and interviews were being set up.

We were supposed to go to graduate school when he came to me with tears, saying, "The Lord is calling me to be a coach and I can't run from it anymore."

I saw my husband's heart surrendering to our heavenly Father's calling upon his life and for our families. I sent him back to the altar three times, you know, just to double, double check.

Fast forward eighteen years, and we're still doing this coaching life, now as a family of four. We've experienced rainouts, strong winds, power outages, and even a couple tornadoes. Throughout it all Jesus Christ has been our guiding light in the darkest nights and brightest days.

This playbook offers strategies, practices, and stories to help you physically walk out your faith while carrying your players to the feet of Jesus. As you boldly step into this sixty-day playbook, you are saying yes to inviting Jesus to walk in front of you and your players. You are saying yes to trying something new. You are saying yes to "coaching with a purpose."

One of my greatest blessings is watching my husband soar in the calling he said yes to when the Lord spoke to him. We are nobodies, but with Christ we become somebodies with a purpose. I've walked beside him as his number one fan, field hand, concession stand worker, smack talker, assistant coach, etc., but most importantly, his prayer partner. We've held each other with tears flowing, crying out for each and every player that's ever said, "Coach Hodges."

When you fully grasp your purpose in the Lord as a coach, everything changes! Yes, you love to see the wins come, but know that there will also be losses.

*Coaching with a Purpose* will help you in your calling as a coach, assisting you to reach players and potentially their families, connecting on a level that becomes transformational off and on the playing surfaces.

This playbook is broken down into Preseason, Season, and Postseason. The Preseason is laying the foundation for your whole season. Remember, in preseason games you work out any kinks while also returning to the "Game Ready" poster. Here you will dig deep quickly, grabbing hold of who God is calling you personally to be as a coach today. No matter your time in coaching, allow this week to speak and grow you.

When you move into a Season, there will be five days a week broken down into ten to twenty minutes each day. You will be asked to physically walk out an action of guided journaling, prayer walking, or fasting. This comes from learning that every miracle Jesus performed in His ministry required an action of movement towards Him.

Wrapping up the regular Season brings you to the Postseason Tournament. Going for the Gold, the Gold that streets are made of, that is! You know wins and losses come; that's part of sports. The victories in this playbook will NEVER be erased next season; they are ETERNAL, written forever in the Lamb's Book of Life by the blood of Jesus.

## Note to Coaches:

The goal is to supply quick reads with actions of prayer walking, fasting, or journaling in ways a coach can read through during a busy season while making time to meet with Jesus wherever they are.

As we reflect on stories throughout this playbook, all names and locations have been changed to protect the privacy of all parties.

# Protecting Home Plate

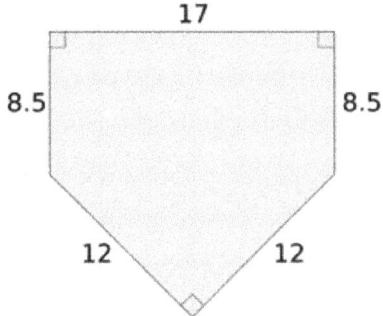

Absolutely EVERYTHING you do from start to finish is built on the gospel of Jesus Christ. The word "gospel" means "good news." It's the good news message that mankind can be saved from the penalty of their sin and receive eternal life in heaven with God through the death, burial, and resurrection of the Lord Jesus Christ.

You protect home plate at all cost in live play. You throw your body in front of every ball that is hurled your way, blocking it with your glove and armor. As you move through this playbook, you will be protecting your home plate at all costs. Your home plate is your team's prayer roster, and your armor is the Armor of God. Now, step into who God is calling you to be as a coach with a purpose beyond the boundaries!

Take a moment to examine your heart. You may remember the joy of when you asked and received Jesus into your heart, or this could all be new to you. Asking Jesus to be the Lord of your life is the greatest decision you will ever make. Reading through "the four," ask Jesus to speak to you in remembrance of your salvation day or to make clear the promise of the gospel through Him and Him alone.

The first seven days of this playbook is your "preseason workout." You will physically walk through the three foundational tools that will be used weekly from here on. Remember preseason training! Your three foundational tools will be journaling, prayer walking, and fasting in the Lord. Each one of these brings an element of surrendering fully, emptying yourself of everything.

> *When they could not find a way to do this because of the crowd, they went up on the roof and lowered him on his mat through the tiles into the middle of the crowd, right in front of Jesus. When Jesus saw their faith, he said, "Friend, your sins are forgiven." (Luke 5:19–20 NIV)*

Coach, today you have the opportunity to walk an uncommon road with every player that crosses your path. You have the opportunity to place your players right in front of Jesus through the power of prayer! Just like the paralyzed man's friends, when in faith they took it upon themselves to find a way to place their friend in front of Jesus to be healed, you are, in a similar way, doing the same with your players through your prayers.

> *It was coaching year fourteen when we randomly ran into a player's dad named Mark in the vegetable aisle at a local grocery store. It had to be the Holy Spirit because none of us eats vegetables, LOL. Mark stood there with a buggy full of food for days with teenagers at home. We visited for a half an hour, talking about his family, then eventually giving hugs as we said our goodbyes. A few days later, my husband received a phone call asking him to come see this dad. He agreed! This was a hard day for our family. We learned that day that my mother-in-love had been diagnosed with breast cancer for the second time. We gathered our strength, praying together to go, because he really wanted to visit with Coach Hodges face to face. As we walked in, tears were flowing, and we had no idea what the Holy Spirit had been up to in the days since we last saw Mark. It was in that vegetable aisle that the Holy Spirit did move: the buggy full of groceries was for his kids to have food for the next week, as he was planning on taking his life that night. As he walked out of the grocery store, he felt the Holy Spirit speak to him. He said, "I want what Coach Hodges and his family has!" That night, face to face, my husband and Mark got*

*down on their knees and prayed together as he accepted Jesus Christ as his personal Lord and Savior. Still to this day, Mark is living a life as the dad Christ has called him to be.*

In this story with Mark and my husband, Mark saw and felt the love of Jesus through our love for his kids, and ultimately wanted that too. Which led to his salvation, and thus the growth of his family's walk with Jesus.

- Are you wanting to see Jesus move?
- Will you seek Him above the crowds and noise?
- Are you willing to humble yourself to Jesus no matter the opposition before you? Opposition can be good or bad.

*Dear heavenly Father, I come to You right now humbly laying my coaching career, players, and any area of play I am in at Your feet, Lord. I ask You to reveal anything unclean to me that's holding me back from fully walking out where You have called me. I surrender it at Your feet, Jesus. Guide my heart as I boldly step into coaching with a purpose, fully surrounded. Jesus, I ask You to fill me with Your wisdom as it says in James to ask for when lacking. I ask You to grant me discernment with every player, seeing past their outward appearance. I ask You to grant me the ability to be strong enough to be gentle as I walk out this playbook. Lord, allow me to see Your hand move, if only from the bleachers; allow me to see Your great and mighty work. Protect me from any and all attacks the devil tries to throw my way. I stand boldly on the blood of Jesus proclaiming victory over the depths of hell. I ask all of these things in the name of Jesus. Amen.*

# The Gospel

## 1. God Loves YOU!

*So God created mankind in his own image, in the image of God he
created them; male and female he created them.*
*(Genesis 3:16)*

*For God so loved the world that he gave his one and only Son, that
whoever believes in him shall not perish but have eternal life.*
*(John 3:16)*

## 2. Sin Separates You.

*For all have sinned and fall short of the glory of God.*
*(Romans 3:23)*

*For the wages of sin is death,*
*but the gift of God is eternal life in Christ Jesus our Lord.*
*(Romans 6:23)*

*But your iniquities have separated you from your God; your sins have
hidden his face from you, so that he will not hear.*
*(Isaiah 59:2)*

## 3. Jesus Rescues You!

*For Christ also suffered once for sins,*
*the righteous for the unrighteous, to bring you to God. He was put to
death in the body but made alive in the Spirit.*
*(I Peter 3:18)*

*I passed on to you what was most important and what had also been passed on to me. Christ died for our sins, just as the Scriptures said. He was buried, and he was raised from the dead on the third day, just as the Scriptures said. He was seen by Peter and then by the twelve. After that, he was seen by more than 500 of his followers at one time, most of whom are still alive, though some have died. Then he was seen by James and later by all the apostles. Last of all, as though I had been born at the wrong time, I also saw him.*
*(1 Corinthians 15:3-8 NLT)*

## 4. Will YOU trust Jesus?

You can place your trust in Jesus by faith through prayer.

Prayer is simply having a conversation with God. God knows your heart and is not concerned with your words as much as he is with the attitude of your heart. Here is a suggested prayer to accept Jesus as your personal Lord and Savior today.

*Dear Lord Jesus, I know that I am a sinner, and I ask for your forgiveness. I believe you died for my sins and rose from the dead. I turn from my sins and invite you to come into my heart and life. I want to trust and follow you as my Lord and Savior. Thank you for loving me and wanting the best for my life.*

*In Jesus name I pray, Amen!*

# PRESEASON

# Jesus Forgives and Heals a Paralyzed Man

One day Jesus was teaching, and Pharisees and teachers of the law were sitting there. They had come from every village of Galilee and from Judea and Jerusalem. And the power of the Lord was with Jesus to heal the sick. Some men came carrying a paralyzed man on a mat and tried to take him into the house to lay him before Jesus. When they could not find a way to do this because of the crowd, they went up on the roof and lowered him on his mat through the tiles into the middle of the crowd, right in front of Jesus.

When Jesus saw their faith, he said, "Friend, your sins are forgiven."

The Pharisees and the teachers of the law began thinking to themselves, "Who is this fellow who speaks blasphemy? Who can forgive sins but God alone?"

Jesus knew what they were thinking and asked, "Why are you thinking these things in your hearts? Which is easier: to say, 'Your sins are forgiven,' or to say, 'Get up and walk'? But I want you to know that the Son of Man has authority on earth to forgive sins." So, he said to the paralyzed man, "I tell you, get up, take your mat and go home." Immediately he stood up in front of them, took what he had been lying on and went home praising God. Everyone was amazed and gave praise to God. They were filled with awe and said, "We have seen remarkable things today." (Luke 5:17–26 NIV)

# Day 1 – Dirty Hands

*When they could not find a way to do this because of the crowd, they went up on the roof and lowered him on his mat through the tiles into the middle of the crowd, right in front of Jesus. When Jesus saw their faith, he said, "Friend, your sins are forgiven."*
*(Luke 5:19–20 NIV)*

As they lowered their friend to Jesus's feet, their hands became dirty. With every miracle Jesus performed, He required the recipient to physically walk something out. The very first miracle when Jesus turned water into wine at the wedding in Cana of Galilee, the recipient had to pour it. And now we're looking at a man being healed by his friends' faith. Jesus told him, "GET UP and WALK." Jesus wants to see our feet in movement towards Him. Jesus wants to see you bringing your players to His feet desperately seeking His healing.

To get their friend to Jesus's feet, it required them to dig through a rooftop and lower him down with ropes, working together. Did they wear gloves? Did their hands get hurt? They didn't look at the cost of getting their friend to Jesus's feet; they did whatever was necessary. As you look at your team, are you willing to share the gospel no matter what the cost (good or bad)?

Take a moment and write out your purpose for coaching. If you just accepted Jesus as your personal Lord and Savior, welcome to the family! You just made the greatest decision of your life!

Maybe you've been coaching for years and know Jesus, so this is a time of reflection. You might need a restart/rest moment with Jesus. Use this opportunity to give Jesus time to speak to you.

No matter where you're coming from, step out of your comfort zone in an uncommon way, allowing Jesus a time to show unconditional love to you and everyone on your team. In the uncommonness, there you'll find the never-ending love of Jesus.

Think of working on a baseball/softball field after a storm. It's a mess! How much time do you put in trying to make it "game ready"? This playbook is going to look like a storm at times as your hands will get dirty. Don't stop! Think back to the friends who lowered the man on the mat. Jesus is right there in the midst. You're taking your players to our heavenly Father's feet.

In the overflowing of your prayers, know Jesus is meeting you there. Jesus loves even the smallest of details. Give Him the details of the players you're taking before Him. Position your players to receive Jesus in His fullness.

Every day, you have the opportunity to make deposits into their lives. We know sometimes these deposits are deposits of correction. When Jesus used correction, it was always followed by a moment of teaching. For the deposits of correction to flow and to allow the needed growth opportunity, there has to be a bank of trust, grace, and love built. Every day that ends in "Y," strive to make a healthy deposit.

# Day 2 - Letting Faith Be First

The friends of the paralyzed man didn't show up at this house unprepared to get their friend to Jesus. They brought the needed supplies to climb, dig, and lower their friend to the feet of Jesus. They prepared for the task before them!

*"When they could not find a way to do this because of the crowd, they went up on the roof and lowered him on his mat through the tiles into the middle of the crowd, **right in front of Jesus**. When Jesus saw their faith, he said, 'Friend, your sins are forgiven'"*
*(Luke 5:19–20 NIV, emphasis mine).*

They lowered their friend right in front of Jesus!

As you build your prayer roster, you're going to be lowering them right in front of Jesus, too. A prayer roster is built by adding everyone on your team, from players to team managers (this could even include the coaching staff). This is where you name them one by one. No one knows their team better than you. As you build your roster, depending on your team size, I recommend putting them in groups of five or ten.

Build your roster in an order that mixes up your team. Remember, you're asking Jesus to show up and show off in an uncommon way. Take a moment to rest in prayer. Ask our heavenly Father to show you the order to build your Coach's Prayer Roster (CPR).

There is also a guide to help you break down specific categories to aid in digging into the details of their lives. Use the guide card for ideas to fill in the blanks on the Coach's Prayer Card. There is also a blank card you can fill out to meet your needs specifically. Get creative. Don't allow fear to hold you back from asking BIG things!

By building your personal prayer roster, you are showing up prepared! You can dig in wherever Jesus leads you, and you will have the ability to lower or raise your team wherever needed.

# Coach's Prayer Roster
## #CPR

| Player | Spiritual | Education | Family | Athletics |
|--------|-----------|-----------|--------|-----------|
|        |           |           |        |           |
|        |           |           |        |           |
|        |           |           |        |           |
|        |           |           |        |           |
|        |           |           |        |           |
|        |           |           |        |           |
|        |           |           |        |           |
|        |           |           |        |           |
|        |           |           |        |           |
|        |           |           |        |           |

| Spiritual | Education | Family | Athletics |
|---|---|---|---|

**Spiritual**

S1: Salvation (John 3:16)

S2: Purpose (Jer. 29:11-13; Psa. 139:13-16; 2 Cor. 5:20; Jer. 1:5; John 14:13; Romans 8:28-29)

S3: Purity (John 8:32; 1 Peter 1:5; Heb. 13:14; 1 Cor. 6:18; 1 John 4:4; James 1:12-14)

S4: Friendships (1 Cor. 15:33; Heb. 10:25; 1 Thess. 5:11; 1 Samuel 16:7)

**Education**

E1: Knowledge (Pro. 1:7; 9:10)

E2: Protection (Psa. 91:2)

E3: Wisdom (James 1:5)

E4: Opportunity (Gal. 5:13; 6:10)

**Family**

F1: God to be guide and guard their family. (Exodus 33:15)

F2: Willingness to go to Jesus in prayer. (Matt. 19:14)

F3: For their parents. (Pro. 22:6)

F4: For good health. (Exodus 23:25)

F5: Dedicated to serving the Lord as a family. (Joshua 24:15)

F6: For their financial needs to be met. (Phil 4:19)

F7: Vision

**Athletics**

A1: Character (James 1:4)

A2: Passion (Col. 3:23)

A3: Humility (1 Thess. 5:17)

A4: Unity/Good Sportsmanship (1 Peter 3:8; 1 Cor. 9:25)

A5: Determination (1 Cor. 15:58; 1 Cor. 7:37)

A6: Strength (Isa. 40:29, 31; Luke 10:27; Eph. 6:10)

A7: Wisdom (Psa. 111:10; Pro. 2:6; Luke 2:40)

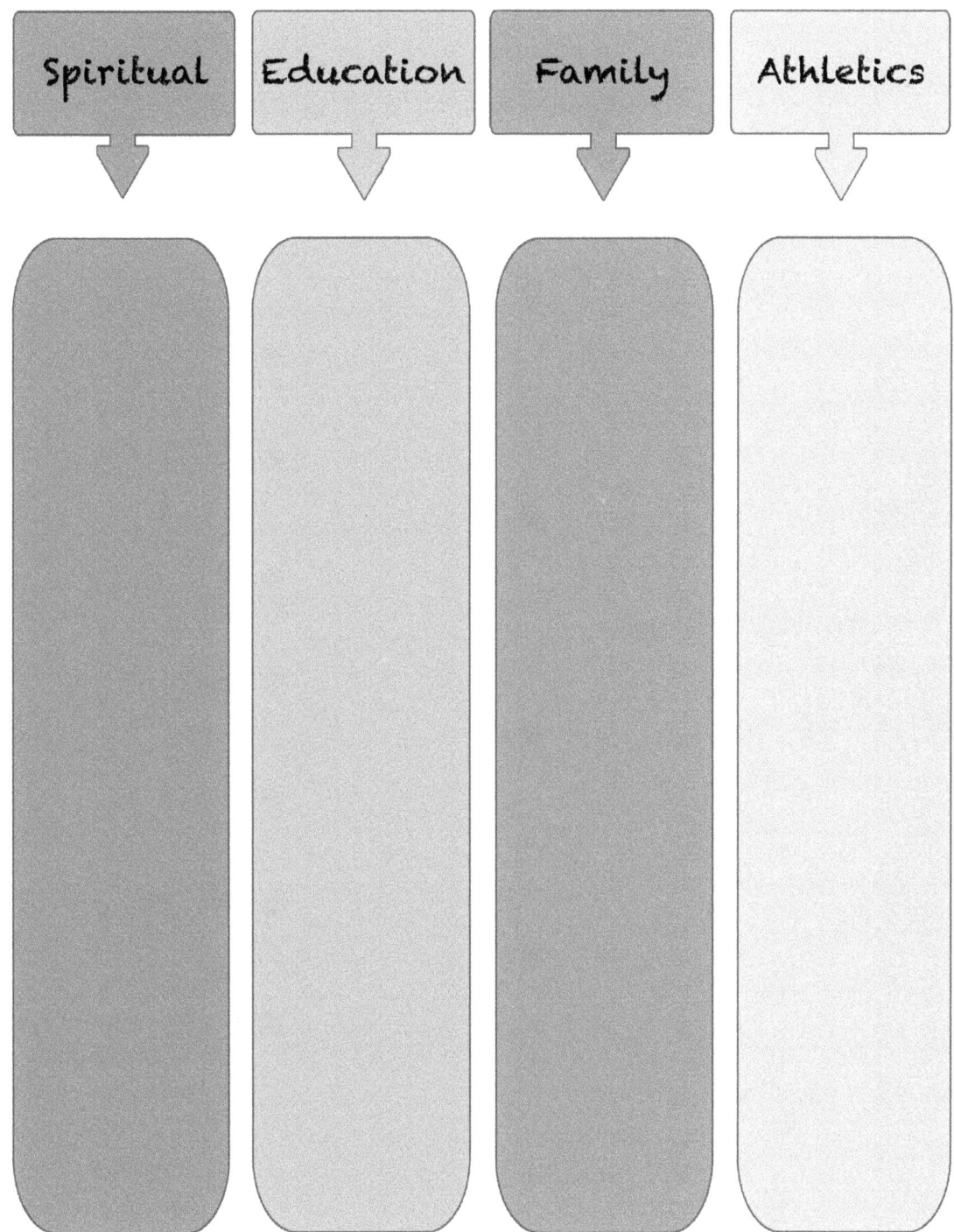

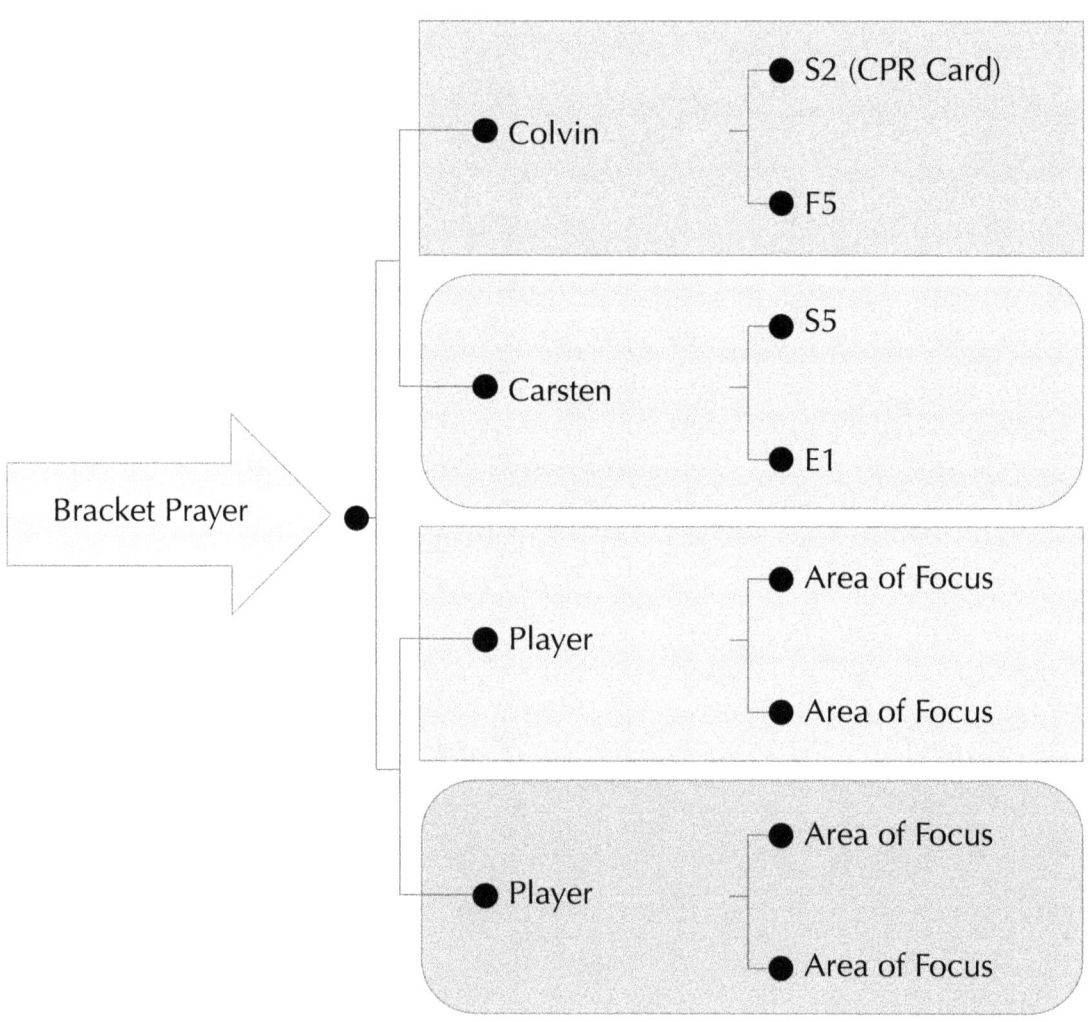

# Day 3 – GET UP / Prayer Walking

One summer my life was forever changed by the power of prayer walking. Every morning for a summer, no matter rain or shine, I prayer walked the fields at my husband's school. That summer, doors were opened for a young ladies' Bible study. We planned to meet once a week, but we ended up meeting twice a week that summer. This carried over into the school year and parents joined by helping meet the needs of feeding the ladies. I saw the Lord move mountains that had never been called out before. The head softball coach led the way for her team by saying yes to walking out and getting baptized. The season ended with eternal victories that will never be forgotten and changed the course of generations to come from these young ladies.

Know there is power in EVERY step of prayer you take on your field, Coach!

> Then Jesus said to him, "**GET UP! Pick up your mat and walk.**"
> At once the man was cured; he picked up his mat and walked.
> (John 5:8–9 NIV, emphasis mine)

The gospel of John goes right to *"GET UP! Pick up your mat and walk."* As Jesus requires movement towards Him in all of His miracles, today, GET UP! Stand fully in who Jesus has called you to be as a coach. Start walking today in the uncommon love Jesus has lavished upon you and praying your prayer roster with confidence knowing Jesus will meet you there.

What is prayer walking?

> *Prayer walking is a type of intercessory prayer that involves walking to or near a particular place while praying. As you prayer walk, your prayers extend beyond your own concerns, focusing directly*

> *on the needs of others and opening yourself to see them with*
> *God's eyes and heart.*                                                — *C.S. Lewis*

Today, take your prayer roster directly to Jesus by walking it out in your game area.

- Baseball/softball: walk the bases.
- Basketball: count the lines.
- Football: walk the yards.
- Track/field: measure the distance.
- Water polo: swim the laps.

Take time to pray over everyone on your roster by name. It might be five minutes or 121 minutes; no matter the time, knowing Jesus is meeting you there is humbling.

## Example of Prayer Walking on a Baseball/ Softball Field:

## PRAY

- <u>Home plate to 1st base</u> = **P**raise Jesus for all He is doing in your life.
- <u>1st to 2nd</u> = **R**epent. Ask for forgiveness in any and all areas the Holy Spirit brings to mind.
- <u>2nd to 3rd</u> = **A**sk Jesus for the desires of your heart. Ask for victories on and off the playing surfaces. Ask for eternal WINS.
- <u>3rd to home plate</u> = **Y**ield to God speaking back to you. Stop and pray, "Lord, speak to me, for I am listening."

> *Dear heavenly Father, thank You for meeting me where I am*
> *today physically, mentally, and spiritually. As I step out boldly in*
> *covering this coaching surface in prayers, I ask You to move in*
> *abundance here. I am surrendering it all to You, Lord. Have Your*
> *way here. Grant us victories on and off this surface. May the lives*

*of the players you have entrusted me with, and their families, be forever changed in and through Your name, Jesus. May they see Jesus above it all. Grant me the ability to coach and lead as You've called me to. Fill me with Your wisdom as I walk this surface. May I be slow to anger, quick to listen, and able to adjust with grace.*

# Day 4 - Fasting / Strengthening Your Intimacy with God

We see throughout the Old and New Testament eras and during the last two thousand years that fasting has been a primary means of humbling ourselves before God. Fasting is interlaced from Esther to Jesus Himself. It is voluntary and total abstinence from food (or other things) for a set amount of time or days; it's a means to devote oneself to prayer and seeking God. Jesus's fasting can be read in one major occasion in Matthew 4:1–11 (NIV).

> *Then Jesus was led by the Spirit into the wilderness to be tempted by the devil. After fasting forty days and forty nights, he was hungry. The tempter came to him and said, "If you are the Son of God, tell these stones to become bread." Jesus answered, "It is written: 'Man shall not live on bread alone, but on every word that comes from the mouth of God.'" Then the devil took him to the holy city and had him stand on the highest point of the temple. "If you are the Son of God," he said, "throw yourself down. For it is written: 'He will command his angels concerning you, and they will lift you up in their hands, so that you will not strike your foot against a stone.'" Jesus answered him, "It is also written: 'Do not put the Lord your God to the test.'" Again, the devil took him to a very high mountain and showed him all the kingdoms of the world and their splendor. "All this I will give you," he said, "if you will bow down and worship me." Jesus said to him, "Away from me, Satan! For it is written: 'Worship the Lord your God, and serve him only.'" Then the devil left him, and angels came and attended him.*

Fasting and prayer work! Together they move the immovable mountains. By combining prayer and fasting, the results can be remarkable. It's a moment only God Himself can grant. Here we learn:

- In Nehemiah 9, God welcomed Israel back into His arms.

- In Esther 4:16, King Xerxes spared Esther when he had every right to kill her for approaching the throne uninvited. He listened to her, and he helped her rescue Israel from Haman.
- In Daniel 9, God hears Daniel's pleas and sends an angel to prophesy to him.
- In Psalm 35:12–14, David doesn't materially gain from praying and fasting for his enemies—quite the opposite, actually—but he reveals to the world that he truly is a man after God's own heart.
- In Luke 2:36–38, Anna gets to meet her Savior in person.
- In Acts 14:23, Paul and Barnabas found the men God wanted them to appoint as elders.

Even if you don't see the results you're seeking through fasting and prayer, don't stop. Seeing the hardships David faced in his life wasn't enough to stop him, so why are your hardships enough to stop you? Faceplant into Jesus!

Learning to discern the results, just as our heroes from biblical times had to do, will hopefully encourage you to make prayer and fasting a staple in your life. Jesus tells us in the New Testament how we should conduct ourselves when fasting. He doesn't say, "If you fast," but says, "When you fast" (see Matthew 6:16–18). When you fast, seeking Jesus, your intimacy level grows tremendously in your relationship with Him.

*I am the bread of life. Whoever comes to me will never go hungry, and whoever believes in me will never be thirsty. (John 6:35 NIV)*

*You know that the testing of your faith produces perseverance. (James 1:3 NIV)*

*And when you fast, do not look gloomy … anoint your head and wash your face, that your fasting may not be seen by others but by your Father who is in secret. And your Father who sees in secret will reward you. (Matthew 6:16–18 ESV)*

*So I say, walk by the Spirit, and you will not gratify the desires of the flesh. (Galatians 5:16 NIV)*

*At once the Spirit sent him out into the wilderness, and he was in the wilderness forty days, being tempted by Satan. He was with the wild animals, and angels attended him. (Mark 1:12–13 NIV)*

*Pray that you may not fall into temptation. (Luke 22:40 NIV)*

*"Even now," declares the Lord, "return to me with all your heart, with fasting and weeping and mourning." (Joel 2:12 NIV)*

*Finally, be strong in the Lord and in the strength of his might. Put on the whole armor of God... (Ephesians 6:10–11 NIV)*

## During the Fast

During your fast, set aside specific and significant time to worship and seek God in prayer. Plan ahead so your time can be unhurried, and conducive to enjoying the Lord. Before starting, take time to sit in prayer by repenting of any sins the Holy Spirit brings to mind and ask for God's forgiveness.

Moving forward, while studying this playbook, every Wednesday set aside time for fasting over your prayer roster. Take today to prayerfully ask our heavenly Father to show you what He desires you to fast. Each week you will have the opportunity to choose between a traditional fast where you abstain from food for a day, or you may choose a partial fast where you choose to abstain from something specific like soda, social media, TV, etc. No matter which one you choose, choose it fully and walk it out. You ask your players to give their ALL, so give your ALL throughout this playbook. By giving Jesus your ALL, mountains will be moved!

*Dear heavenly Father, thank You for Your unfailing love and understanding. Thank You for meeting me fully where I am. Please reveal anything unclean within me; show me, O Lord. I ask You to remove what is keeping me from walking out who You are calling me to be. Please forgive me when I fail You. Show me, Lord, what I need to fast today to grow in faith. May I grow in understanding and knowledge of You through fasting. Expand my heart, Lord, in showing Your love, mercy, and grace to my players. Grant me a boldness in sharing the gospel with my players. I lay everything I am at Your feet, Lord. Mold me, as I am the clay, and You are the potter. I ask all of this in the name of Jesus. Amen.*

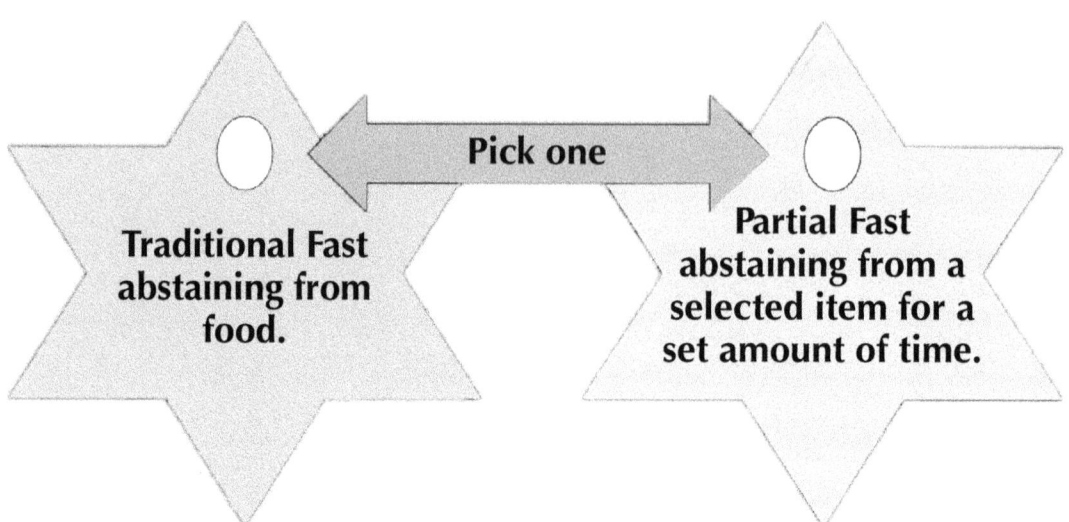

This week I'm fasting......

# Day 5 - Journaling

When we journal, it creates a time for intentional reflection and vulnerability with our heavenly Father. Though the term "journaling" can't be found in Scriptures, we can grasp the many benefits of journaling that enhance your personal walk with Christ. It helps to lay a foundation of reflections of prayers prayed and their answers.

The elegance of journaling is that we are able to bare ourselves before our heavenly Father, pouring out our hearts and fears, while reminding ourselves of the faithful and merciful God we serve.

Throughout this playbook, you will have opportunities to journal weekly. Take that time to truly capture everything down to the smallest detail. Think of journaling as your end-of-season report. You will be able to recap the growth and development within your team and your personal walk with Christ.

We can't find "journaling" in Scripture, but here are a few verses that help pull us towards taking the treasures happening around us and writing them down.

## Mary Pondered God's Promise

*So, they hurried off and found Mary and Joseph, and the baby, who was lying in the manger. When they had seen him, they spread the word concerning what had been told them about this child, and all who heard it were amazed at what the shepherds said to them. **But Mary treasured all these things and pondered them in her heart. The shepherds returned, glorifying and praising God for all the things they had heard and seen, which were just as they had been told.***
*(Luke 2:16–20 NIV, emphasis mine)*

## Remembering God's Wonderful Deeds

*After David had finished sacrificing the burnt offerings and fellowship offerings, he blessed the people in the name of the Lord.*
*(1 Chronicles 16:2 NIV)*

## The People Pondered and Delighted in God's Great Work

*Great are the works of the Lord;*
*they are pondered by all who delight in them. (Psalm 111:2 NIV)*

## Bible Verses on Writing

*Then the Lord replied:*
*"Write down the revelation*
*and make it plain on tablets*
*so that a herald may run with it."*
*(Habakkuk 2:2 NIV)*

*Let love and faithfulness never leave you;*
*bind them around your neck,*
*write them on the tablet of your heart.*
*Then you will win favor and a good name*
*in the sight of God and man. (Proverbs 3:3–4 NIV)*

*This is what the Lord, the God of Israel, says:*
*"Write in a book all the words I have spoken to you."*
*(Jeremiah 30:2 NIV)*

*He who was seated on the throne said,*
*"I am making everything new!" Then he said,*
*"Write this down, for these words are trustworthy and true."*
*(Revelation 21:5 NIV)*

*The revelation from Jesus Christ, which God gave him to show his servants what must soon take place. He made it known by sending his angel to his servant John, who testifies to everything he saw—that is, the word of God and the testimony of Jesus Christ. Blessed is the one who reads aloud the words of this prophecy, and blessed are those who hear it and take to heart what is written in it, because the time is near.*
*(Revelation 1:1–3 NIV)*

*These commandments that I give you today are to be on your hearts. Impress them on your children. Talk about them when you sit at home and when you walk along the road, when you lie down and when you get up. Tie them as symbols on your hands and bind them on your foreheads. Write them on the doorframes of your houses and on your gates.*
*(Deuteronomy 6:6–9 NIV)*

## Verses That Encourage and Give Inspiration

*Keep this Book of the Law always on your lips; meditate on it day and night, so that you may be careful to do everything written in it. Then you will be prosperous and successful.*
*(Joshua 1:8 NIV)*

*When your words came, I ate them;*
*they were my joy and my heart's delight,*
*for I bear your name,*
*Lord God Almighty.*
*(Jeremiah 15:16 NIV)*

*Jesus answered, "It is written: 'Man shall not live on bread alone, but on every word that comes from the mouth of God.'"*
*(Matthew 4:4 NIV)*

*Record my misery;*
*list my tears on your scroll—*
*are they not in your record?*
*(Psalm 56:8 NIV)*

*Do not be anxious about anything, but in every situation, by prayer and*
*petition, with thanksgiving, present your requests to God. And the peace*
*of God, which transcends all understanding, will guard your hearts and*
*your minds in Christ Jesus.*
*(Philippians 4:6–7 NIV)*

*The tongue has the power of life and death,*
*and those who love it will eat its fruit.*
*(Proverbs 18:21 NIV)*

*In the same way, let your light shine before others,*
*that they may see your good deeds and glorify your Father in heaven.*
*(Matthew 5:16 NIV)*

*Because of the Lord's great love we are not consumed,*
*for his compassions never fail.*
*They are new every morning;*
*great is your faithfulness.*
*(Lamentations 3:22–23)*

# THE SEASON

*Let perseverance finish its work*
*so that you may be mature and complete,*
*not lacking anything.*
*(James 1:4 NIV)*

Coach, there's JOY on your playing surfaces as you shout out the praises and promises of the LORD over your team! The preparations have been made, foundations have been laid, and now it is time to put all of your work into action with your team. Let's go!

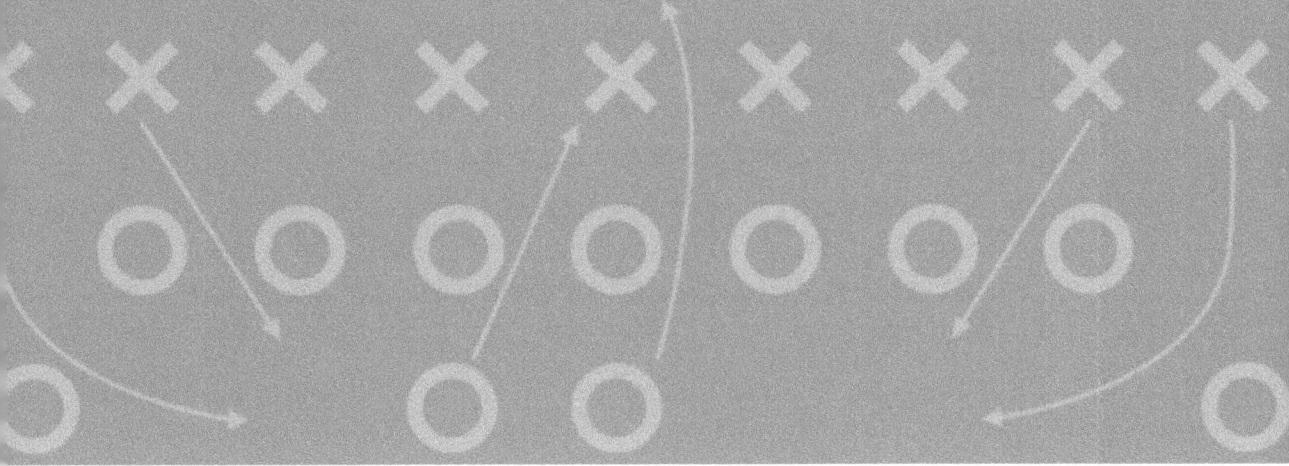

# WEEK 2

*Before I formed you in the womb I knew you; before you were born,*
*I set you apart; I appointed you as a prophet to the nations.*
*(Jeremiah 1:5 NIV)*

Jeremiah was raised in a godly home, but Scripture shows that he had a personal encounter with God. He grasped that God had a calling upon his life before he was even formed. He understood God had handpicked him for a calling higher than he could have ever accomplished on his own strength.

Four times it says "I" in the verse; four times God confirmed He KNEW Jeremiah before he was formed. In the same way, He knew you before you were even a twinkle in anyone's eyes. How does embracing the fact that God knew you before you were even formed in your mother's womb change your approach to God? Knowing that it's not by accident, or random gust of wind that you've landed in your location and coaching field. Grasping that the God of the universe knew every single player you would coach before you even signed the contract. Do you believe?

## Day 6 – Journal / Write out the Bible verse for this week / Build your prayer bracket from your player roster

Coach! You've gotta start somewhere, so why not here? You can't change the past, but you can change the future. Start now! Start here! What is your number one priority? Pour everything you have into Jesus. Faceplant into Him today.

Take time to go meet with your players one-on-one for a moment. Ask them how they are doing this week. Is there anything they would like to get off their chest? Let them know you're listening.

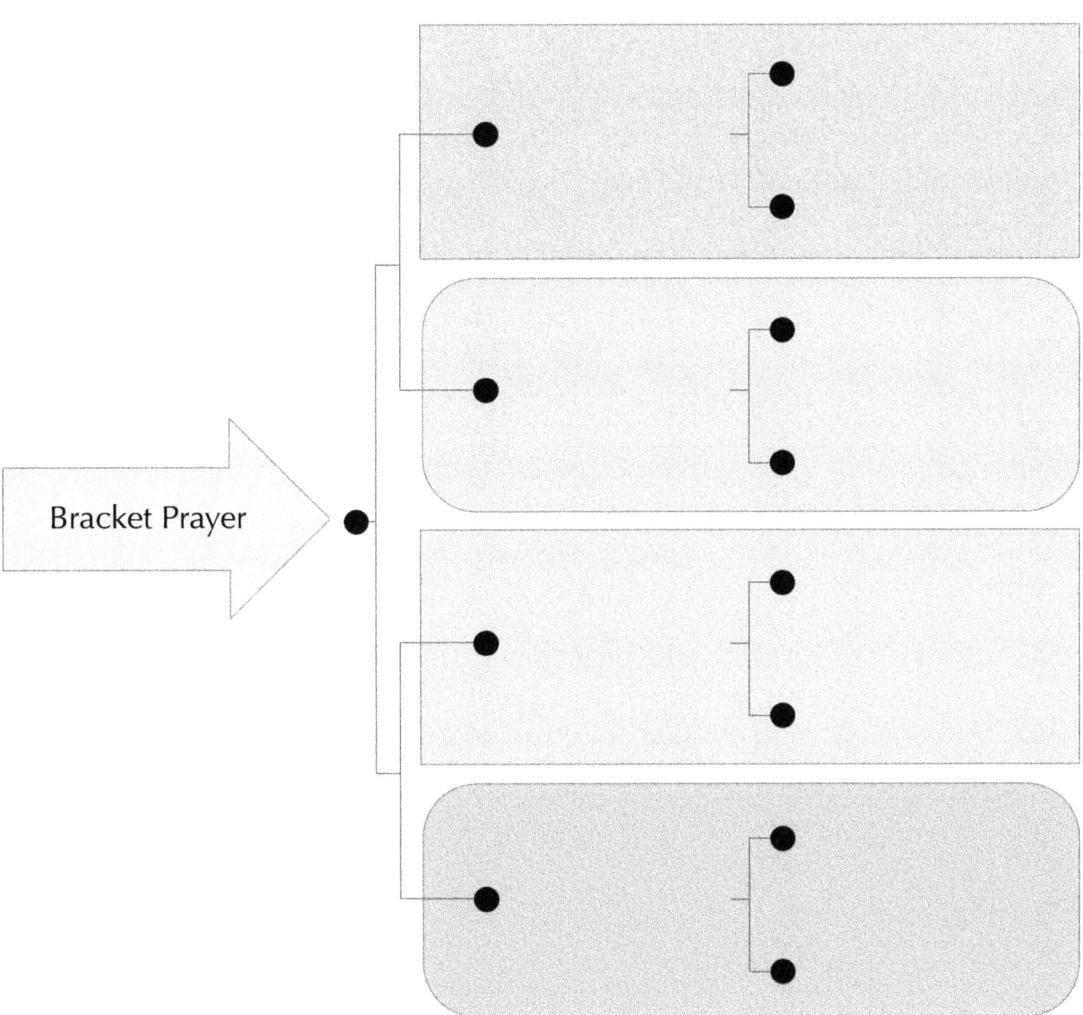

# Day 7 - Prayer Walking

*An open in motion conversation with God.*
*Moving as water through rock in a stream.*
*Becoming fluid with every shifting pebble.*
*– Heather Hodges*

Coach, lace up your shoes! Allow love to break through here as you cry out to Jesus for your players. Take a moment to fill out the chart below as you align **your heart** for prayer walking over the team Jesus handpicked for you.

Ask the Holy Spirit, "What are You saying to me?"

## Prayer Chart

| | |
|---|---|
| **P** - Praise | |
| **R** - Repent | |
| **A** - Ask | |
| **Y** - Yield | |

# Weekly Coach's Prayer Roster

#CPR

| Player | Spiritual | Education | Family | Athletics |
|--------|-----------|-----------|--------|-----------|
|        |           |           |        |           |
|        |           |           |        |           |
|        |           |           |        |           |
|        |           |           |        |           |
|        |           |           |        |           |
|        |           |           |        |           |
|        |           |           |        |           |
|        |           |           |        |           |
|        |           |           |        |           |
|        |           |           |        |           |

# Day 8 - Fasting

Years ago, I committed to a ten-day traditional fast with a team. To be honest, I was scared. Mostly, my fear stemmed from being afraid of failure because I am a picky eater! Like toddler-picky! I took time to prepare food ahead in anticipation of what the Lord was going to do. Fasting can be intimidating, but only if you allow it to be. Know that God is going to meet you there during the process. He is going to embrace you in the journey.

Prepare yourself to be game ready when you walk into a fast. Give God your best, just as you're asking Him to do for you. In my ten-day fast, my intimacy grew deeper with God than it had ever before. I reached my end, and He picked me up! He moved mountains into the sea. After that fast, our family moved across our state. During the moving process, I was okay with moving into a home I hadn't even seen the inside of. God granted me a peace that surpassed all understanding in a world full of unknowns. I want to encourage you to jump in. Give God the opportunity to show you a deeper love.

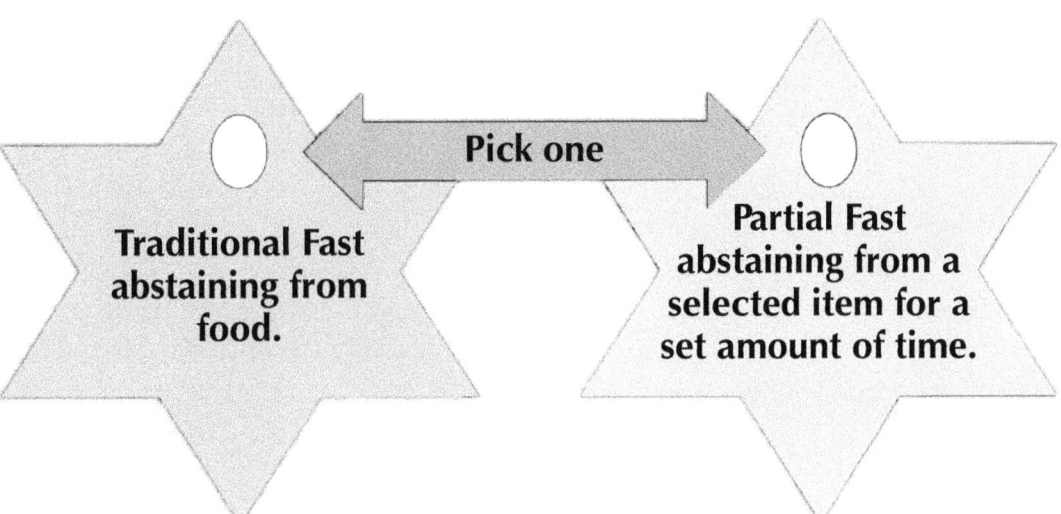

This week I'm fasting......

# Day 9 - Reflection / Yield

*Before I formed you in the womb I knew you; before you were born,*
*I set you apart; I appointed you as a prophet to the nations.*
*(Jeremiah 1:5 NIV)*

Coach, you just completed the first three days of your season in this playbook. Congratulations! Take a moment to reflect over it all. Ask God, "What are You saying to me?" Write it out, in detail.

_____

_____

_____

_____

_____

_____

_____

_____

# Day 10 – Proclaiming victories / Surrendering everything

Chancey landed his very first coaching job at the state tournament in baseball. I remember walking up to the fence and giving him a kiss; he had the biggest smile! He had made it where everyone tries to get at the start of the season. It would be years before he saw it again. To have that taste and not reach it year in and out can get frustrating, especially if you only look at it through the eyes of worldly views. When you step into "coaching with a purpose" through Jesus Christ, it changes you. There is no reset at the end of the season on the eternal victories! They're recorded in the Lamb's Book of Life in the blood of Jesus.

As this week comes to an end, take time to name the victories this week on and off the field.

_____

_____

_____

_____

Was there a mountain you saw moved this week? If so, how is your heart to-wards it today? If not, what is the mountain you're wanting to see moved? Lay it down again and again at the feet of Jesus.

_____

_____

_____

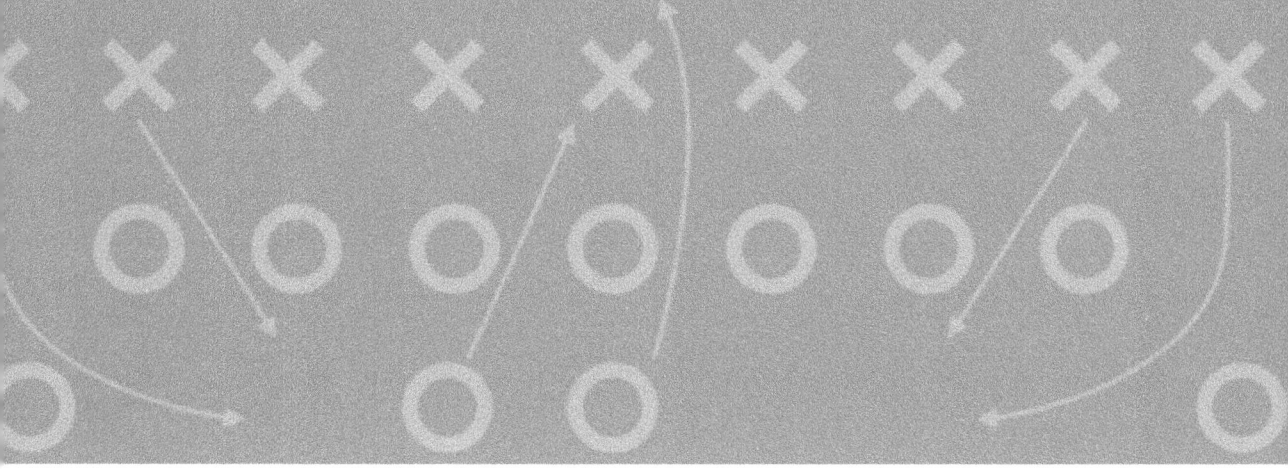

## WEEK 3

*For I know the thoughts that I think toward you, says the Lord, thoughts of peace and not of evil, to give you a future and a hope. Then you will call upon Me and go and pray to Me, and I will listen to you. And you will seek Me and find Me, when you search for Me with all your heart.*
*(Jeremiah 29:11–13 NKJV)*

God, through the prophet Jeremiah in the entire chapter 29, is speaking to the Jews through a letter telling them that He has <u>not</u> abandoned His people. It is His instructions and intentions for them while they are in exile in Babylon. This section, verses 11–13, is a highlight of His love and desire for His people at all times, not just during the "winning seasons," but also the "losing seasons." It's a reminder to always call upon Him and He will see you through it.

# Day 11 - Journal

Take time to build your prayer bracket from your player roster. Lay out your battle plan for the week in detail. You're fighting for your players in the heavenly realms. You could be the VERY first person to ever cover them in prayers. Be bold here! Ask God to move the mountains you see.

Take time to go meet with your players one-on-one for a moment. Ask them how they are doing this week. Is there anything they would like to get off their chest? Let them know you're listening.

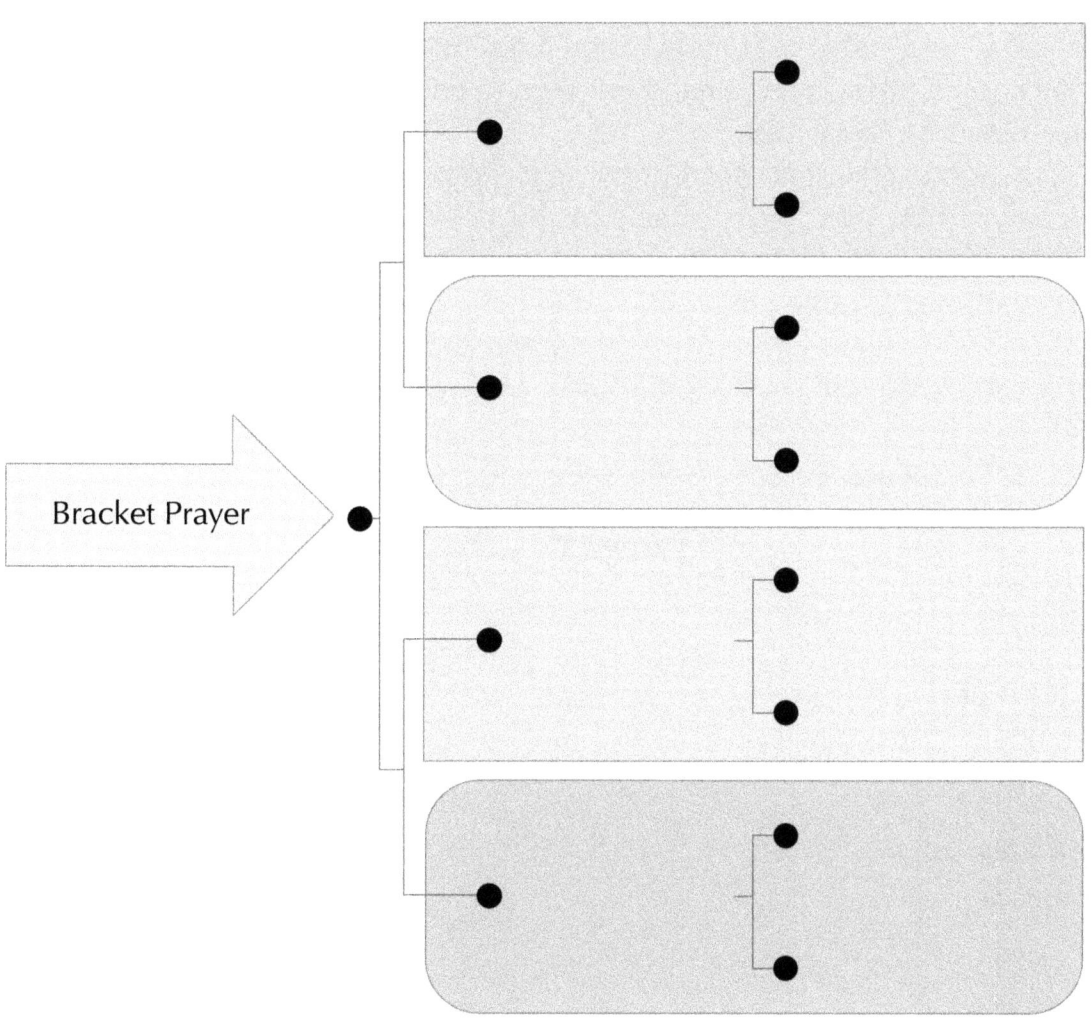

# Day 12 – Prayer Walking

Chancey's very first time coaching football, they went 0-10! Yep, they didn't win a single game. In fact, they had to forfeit HALF of their schedule! To say that was a hard year is an understatement. This was the place I had fasted for and had total peace over moving into a house I had never seen the inside of. We knew God had orchestrated our steps to be here; we trusted Him through the desert we had landed in.

It was in this time God grew us deeper again in His love and intimacy. When you find yourself in the desert, remember the words in Jeremiah: "For I know the thoughts that I think toward you, says the Lord, thoughts of peace and not of evil, to give you a future and a hope. Then you will call upon Me and go and pray to Me, and I will listen to you. And you will seek Me and find Me, when you search for Me with all your heart" (Jer. 29:11–13 NKJV).

As you prayer walk this week, press into Jesus with every step!

## Prayer Chart

| | |
|---|---|
| **P** - Praise | |
| **R** - Repent | |
| **A** - Ask | |
| **Y** - Yield | |

# Day 13 - Fasting

Chancey's third season of coaching football went totally opposite of the first. During this season, they went 9-0! They went from a season of totally losing to winning every game. A lot had changed in the off season: the school had moved to eight-man football, but because they had switched during the district realignment cycle, they were not eligible for playoffs. However, it was evident the future was bright. Besides playing with a different number of players on the field, they were playing on a completely different playing field. Literally, the dimensions changed from 100 yards x 53.3 yards to 100 yards x 40 yards. When you approach Jesus in fasting, the answer can be totally changing your playing field. He can literally change the dimensions that once were holding your back. Be fluid in your mobility; allow Him the freedom to move like water through a stream.

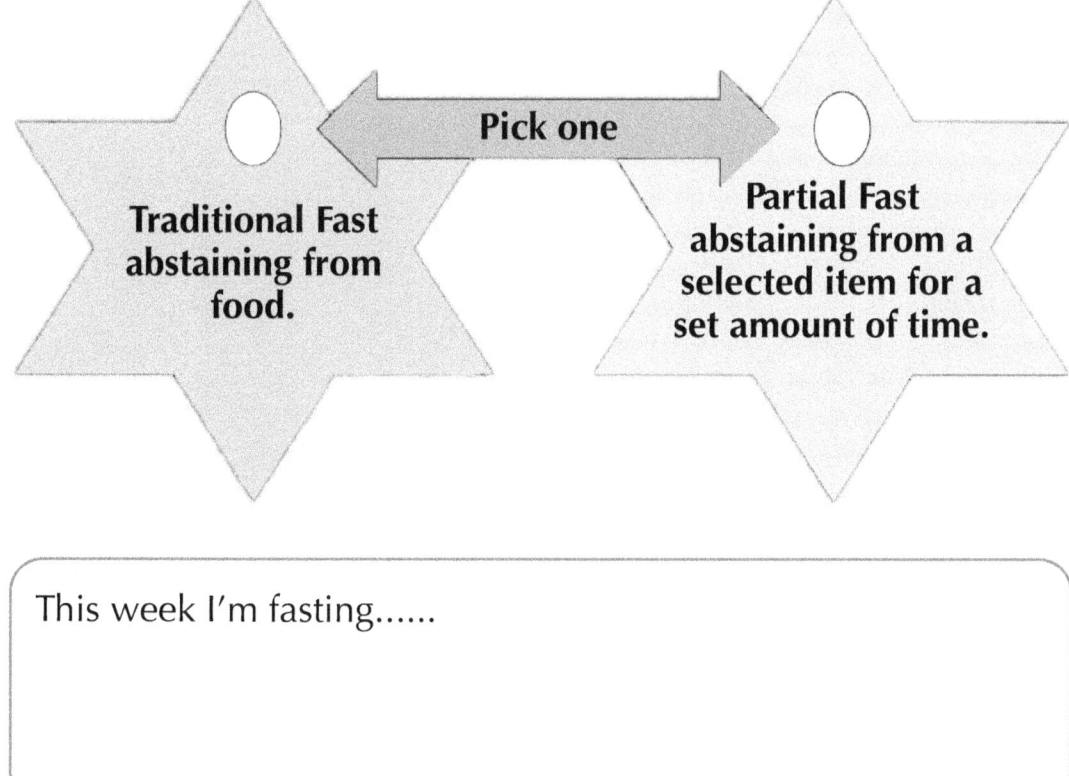

This week I'm fasting......

# Day 14 - Reflection / Yield

*For I know the thoughts that I think toward you, says the Lord, thoughts of peace and not of evil, to give you a future and a hope. Then you will call upon Me and go and pray to Me, and I will listen to you. And you will seek Me and find Me, when you search for Me with all your heart.*
*(Jeremiah 29:11–13 NKJV)*

Take a moment and yield yourself to Jesus as you read these verses.
Ask the Holy Spirit, "What are You telling me this week?" You might be in a hard season, or maybe you haven't lost a game yet. Throw it all at the feet of Jesus! Rest there today.

# Day 15 – Proclaiming victories / Surrendering everything

As this week comes to an end, take time to name the victories this week on and off the field. Go in details. Take time to praise our heavenly Father with every stroke of the pen.

_____

_____

_____

_____

_____

_____

_____

Was there a mountain you saw moved this week? If so, how is your heart towards it today? If not, what is the mountain you're wanting to see moved? Lay it down again and again at the feet of Jesus.

_____

_____

_____

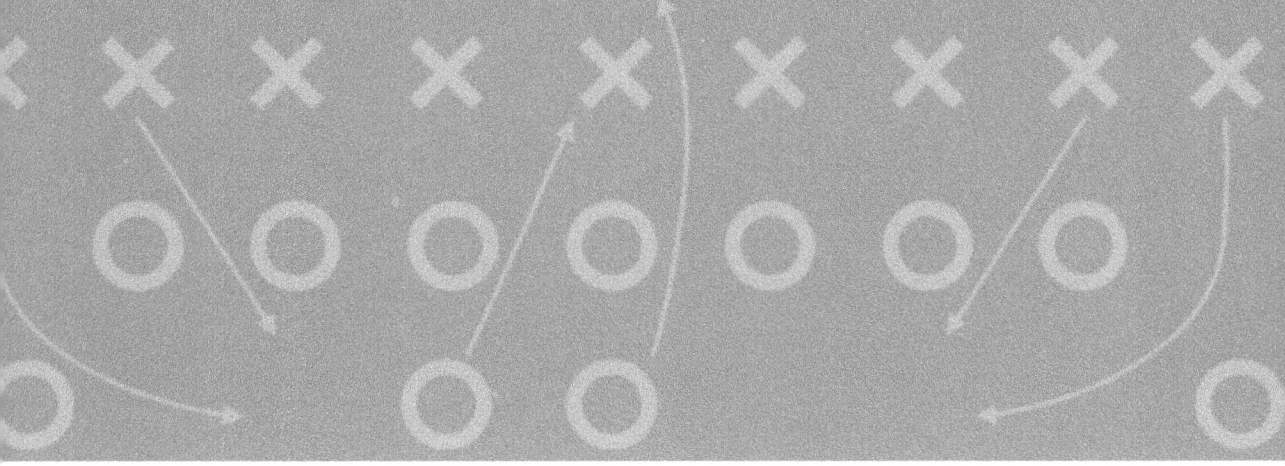

*Dear brothers and sisters, when troubles of any kind come your way, consider it an opportunity for great joy. For you know that when your faith is tested, your endurance has a chance to grow. So let it grow, for when your endurance is fully developed, you will be perfect and complete, needing nothing.*
*(James 1:2–4 NLT)*

Starting in the coaching industry over eighteen years ago, we were young, green, and wet behind the ears. Since then, we've had our share of victories and challenges like skunks on the field to getting fired for taking a stand against injustice. In the Book of James, we learn what it means to grow in endurance. Our endurance isn't built standing on the sidelines of life. It's built in the grind of daily life. I remember the first time Chancey was fired from coaching. It hit hard! We knew we didn't land in that position by accident, but why was this happening? God had been nudging us to move and we were stubborn; our boys were just toddlers at that time and hadn't started school yet. Nonetheless, we kept giving God excuse after excuse of why we couldn't. In one day, God changed our position in an area and forced our hand to stand up for Him. We don't see the chains that are holding us back until we're called to move.

# Day 16 - Journal

This week build your prayer bracket from your player roster on endurance. You might need to adjust a couple names to meet this area. Take an honest look at your team. Who needs to grow in their endurance? Is it you? Is it another coach on your team? Be honest here. If you're needing wisdom, ask God for it. He tells us in James, "If any of you lacks wisdom you should ask God, who gives generously to all without finding fault, and it will be given to you" (Jas. 1:5 NIV).

Take time to go meet with your players one-on-one for a moment. Ask them how are they doing this week. Is there anything they would like to get off their chest? Let them know you're listening.

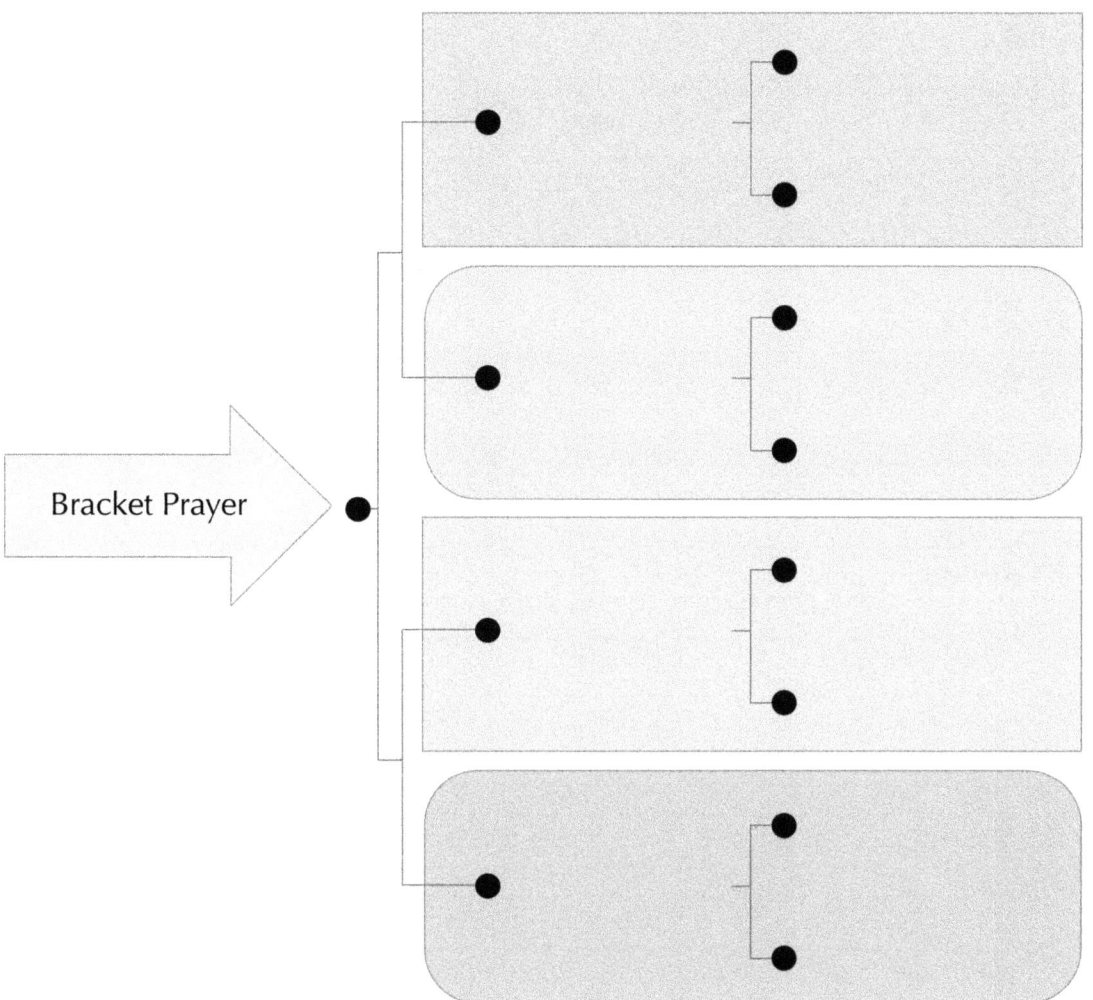

Bracket Prayer

# Day 17 - Prayer Walking

As you walk out prayers this week, ask the Holy Spirit, "What are You showing me?" Center yourself with Jesus today. Allow Him to speak to you in the still quiet whispers. Every step is a step of proclaiming Jesus over your coaching surface.

## Prayer Chart

| | |
|---|---|
| **P** - Praise | |
| **R** - Repent | |
| **A** - Ask | |
| **Y** - Yield | |

# Weekly Coach's Prayer Roster

## #CPR

| Player | Spiritual | Education | Family | Athletics |
|--------|-----------|-----------|--------|-----------|
|        |           |           |        |           |
|        |           |           |        |           |
|        |           |           |        |           |
|        |           |           |        |           |
|        |           |           |        |           |
|        |           |           |        |           |
|        |           |           |        |           |
|        |           |           |        |           |
|        |           |           |        |           |
|        |           |           |        |           |

# Day 18 - Fasting

As we're looking at endurance this week, I want to encourage you to take the next step in fasting if you haven't. Dig a little deeper. If you're physically able to step into the traditional fast this week, give it a try if you haven't yet. You can have broth, water, and juice. Every time your stomach groans for substance, go to Jesus in prayer. Position yourself at His feet, and "pray continually" (1 Thess. 5:17 NIV).

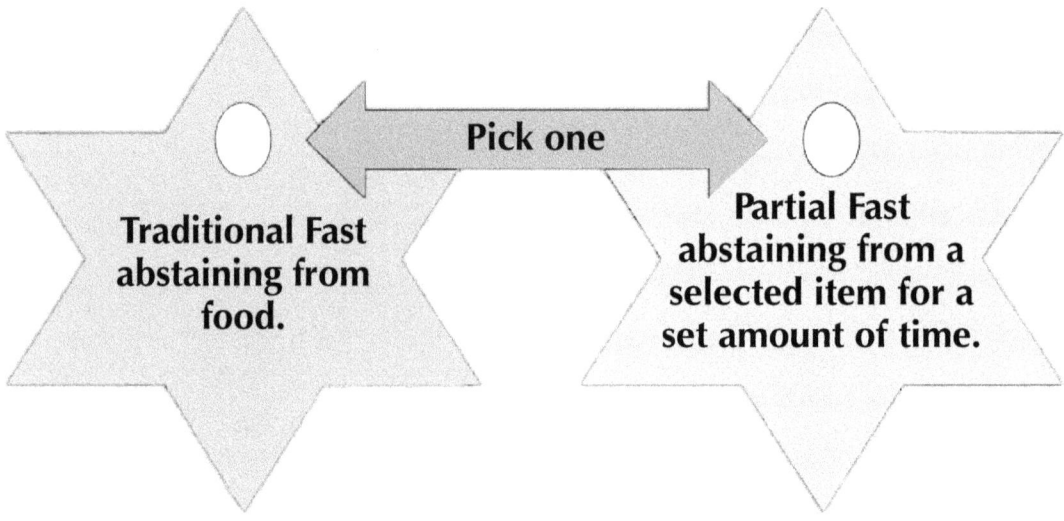

**Pick one**

**Traditional Fast abstaining from food.**

**Partial Fast abstaining from a selected item for a set amount of time.**

This week I'm fasting......

# Day 19 - Reflection / Yield

*Dear brothers and sisters, when troubles of any kind come your way, consider it an opportunity for great joy. For you know that when your faith is tested, your endurance has a chance to grow. So let it grow, for when your endurance is fully developed, you will be perfect and complete, needing nothing.*
*(James 1:2–4 NLT)*

Did endurance come knocking this week? Were you able to see the push to grow and expand in new ways this week? Have you seen players take strides? Remember, growing in endurance could be as simple as keeping your mouth shut when needed.

What did the Holy Spirit show you this week? Give details.

# Day 20 – Proclaiming victories / Surrendering everything

As this week comes to an end, take time to name the victories on and off the field. Go into detail. Take time to praise our heavenly Father with every stroke of the pen.

_____

_____

_____

_____

_____

Was there a mountain you saw moved this week? If so, how is your heart towards it today? If not, what is the mountain you're wanting to see moved? Lay it down again and again at the feet of Jesus.

_____

_____

_____

_____

*Whatever you do [whatever your task may be],*
*work from the soul [that is, put in your very best effort],*
*as [something done] for the Lord and not for men.*
*(Colossians 3:23 AMP)*

During this part of Paul's letter to the church at Colosse, he discusses slaves and masters in the verses leading up to and following this key verse. He does this neither condoning slavery nor is he trying to stir a revolt against the masters. Instead, Paul was laying a level playing field that all are equal in the eyes of God, and that they all should work at all things that they do for the glory of God. Just as you will see or have already seen, Coach, your athletes will try to cut corners and give half effort, leading to poor performance for the team. However, they are doing more than that; they are not putting forth their best efforts to God with the gifts He has given them. Therefore, these verses are an aid in remembering or learning for the first time that ultimately, they are playing for and working for a higher purpose than you. They are doing it all for the highest of the most high, God. And you as their coach are merely a guide to lead them to, remind them of, and propel them towards God's love and mercy.

# Day 21 - Journal

This week, as you build your prayer bracket from your player roster, ask the Holy Spirit, "What are You asking of me?" Write it out in detail.

Take time to go meet with your players one-on-one for a moment. Ask them how they are doing this week. Is there anything they would like to get off their chest? Let them know you're listening.

_____

_____

_____

_____

_____

_____

_____

_____

_____

_____

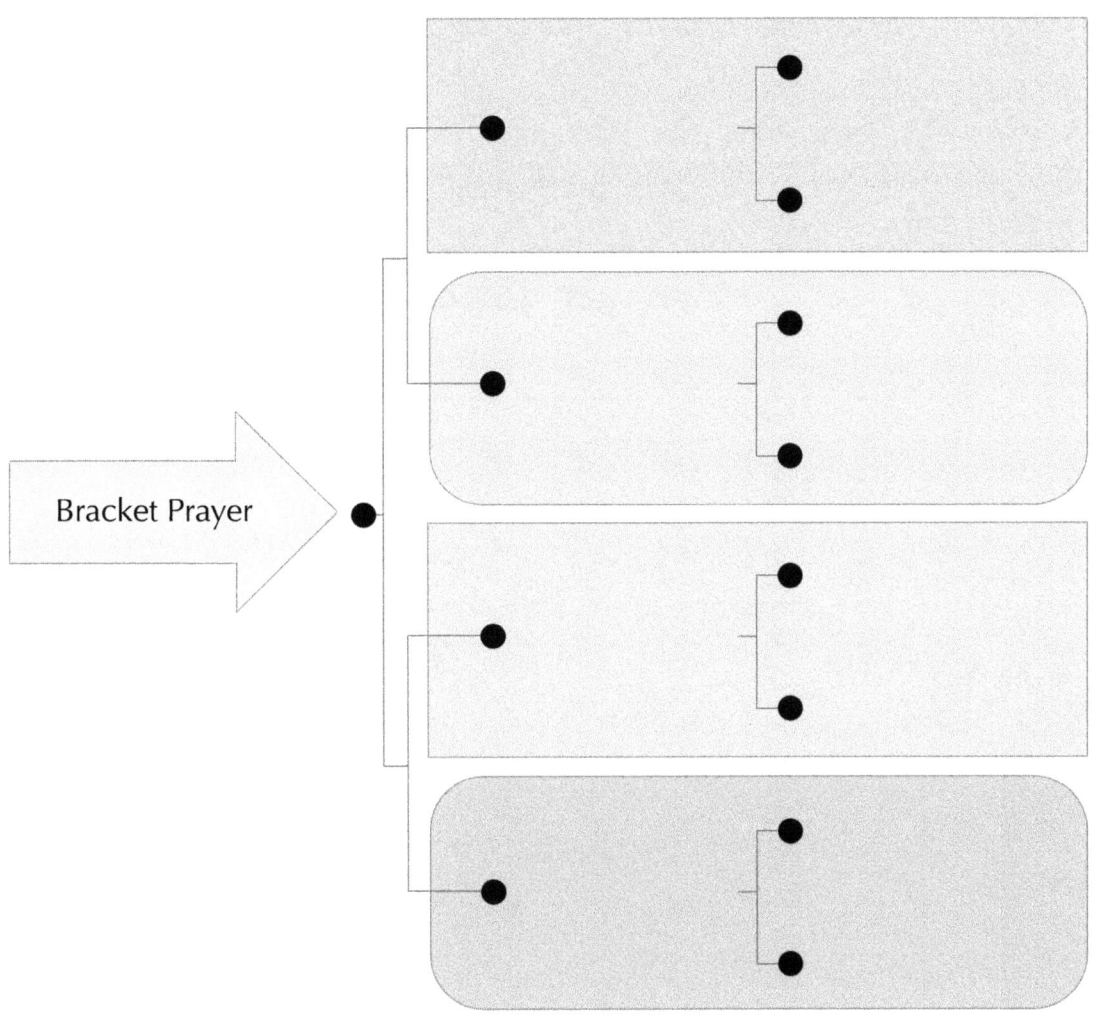

Bracket Prayer

# Day 22 - Prayer Walking

*Whatever you do [whatever your task may be],*
*work from the soul [that is, put in your very best effort],*
*as [something done] for the Lord and not for men.*
*(Colossians 3:23 AMP)*

As you are prayer walking your coaching surface, pray this verse aloud. Proclaim it victoriously. For everything you're doing is not for man, but for our heavenly Father above.

## Prayer Chart

| | |
|---|---|
| **P** - Praise | |
| **R** - Repent | |
| **A** - Ask | |
| **Y** - Yield | |

# Weekly Coach's Prayer Roster

### #CPR

| Player | Spiritual | Education | Family | Athletics |
|---|---|---|---|---|
|  |  |  |  |  |
|  |  |  |  |  |
|  |  |  |  |  |
|  |  |  |  |  |
|  |  |  |  |  |
|  |  |  |  |  |
|  |  |  |  |  |
|  |  |  |  |  |
|  |  |  |  |  |
|  |  |  |  |  |

# Day 23 - Fasting

Last week I challenged you to try traditional fasting if you haven't. This week, the choice is yours. Pray and ask God what it is He wants you to fast.

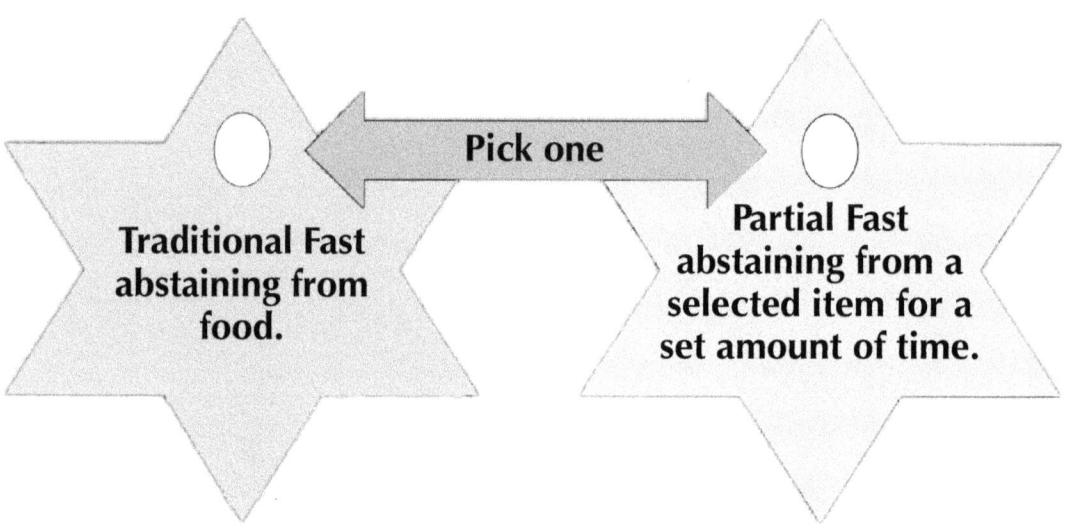

This week I'm fasting......

# Day 24 - Reflection / Yield

How has taking time to meet one-on-one with the players each week been? Have they opened up more to you, sharing what's on their heart? Has it changed your love for them any? Take a moment to think about setting aside this time from now on weekly. How has this changed your coaching?

_____

_____

_____

_____

_____

_____

_____

_____

_____

_____

## Day 25 – Proclaiming victories / Surrendering everything

As this week comes to an end, take time to name the victories on and off the field. Go into detail. Take time to praise our heavenly Father with every stroke of the pen.

_____

_____

_____

_____

_____

_____

Was there a mountain you saw moved this week? If so, how is your heart towards it today? If not, what is the mountain you're wanting to see moved? Lay it down again and again at the feet of Jesus.

_____

_____

_____

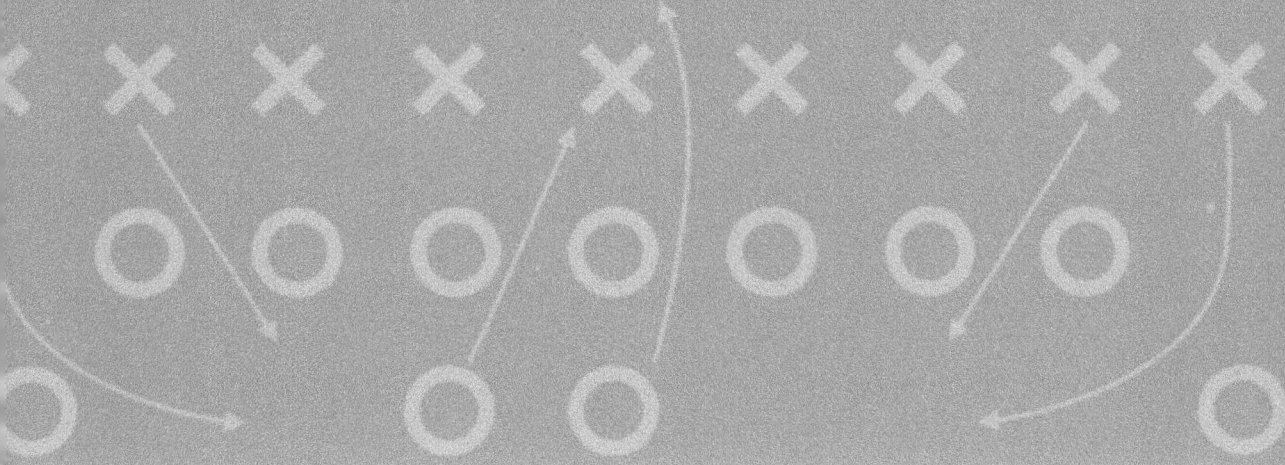

# WEEK 6

*Pray without ceasing.*
*(1 Thessalonians 5:17 NKJV)*

This verse is short yet powerful, bookended by two equally powerful verses. This section of 1 Thessalonians speaks on what to do during the good and hard times of life. Choose joy, speak to God through it all, and be thankful because this is God's will and purpose. Executing this plan of action won't be easy, but during your seasons and especially your life, you will encounter highs and lows, as will your athletes, and the questions about what to do will arise. Psalm 121:1–2 (NIV) says, "I lift my eyes up to the mountains—where does my help come from? My help comes from the Lord, the Maker of heaven and earth." God is there. He is watching. He is waiting. He is there to help. His plans are for our benefit. The answers to the questions can only be answered by talking with God. First Thessalonians tells us what we must do. We must pick up the spiritual telephone and talk to God and do our best to never hang it up again. This open line of communication with God is comforting and reassuring; it is also strengthening and fortifying, because we are going to need it all for the times ahead both on and off the fields of play.

# Day 26 - Journal

Coach, congratulations! You've made it halfway through *Coaching with a Purpose*! I am proud of you! Has your purpose shifted any since day one? Has your approach to your players and coaching surface changed any? Take time to read back through this playbook. Take notes of areas you've seen growth and mountains moved. Remember all the times you were asked to go into detail, and be glad you did. If you didn't, from here on, give it a try. As you read back through, take a highlighter and mark the ones that jump off the page to you; pray them as prayers of thanksgiving to God. Let Him know the JOY you have!

Take time to build your prayer bracket just as you did the weeks before.

Take time to go meet with your players one-on-one for a moment. Ask them how they are doing this week. Is there anything they would like to get off their chest? Let them know you're listening.

_____

_____

_____

_____

_____

_____

_____

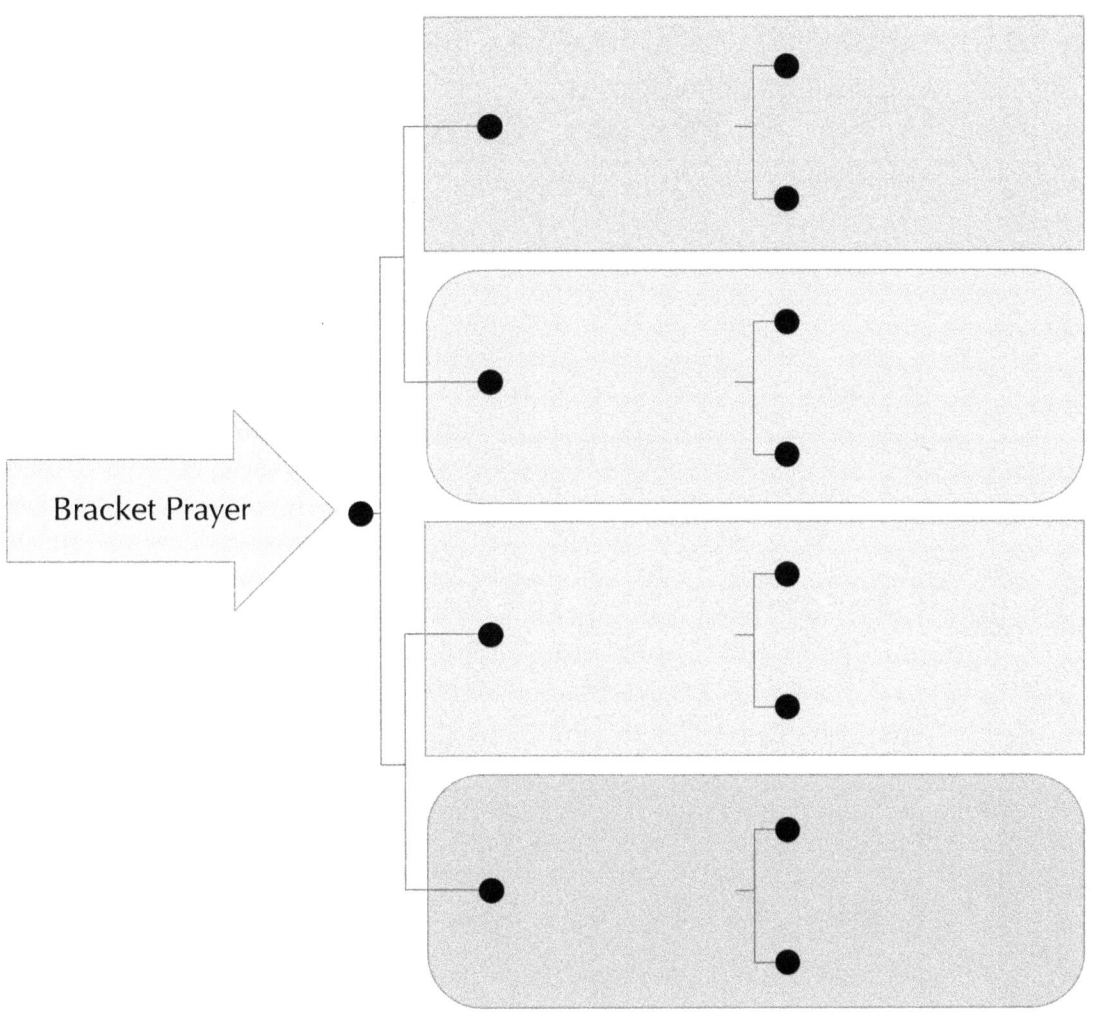

Bracket Prayer

# Day 27- Prayer Walking

This week as you walk your coaching surface, read the things you didn't highlight but were still written out. Offer them as prayers of thanksgiving just as the ones you highlighted. When we pray without ceasing, we release the prayers of thanksgiving, and the ones that keep us on our knees in the darkest hour.

## Prayer Chart

| | |
|---|---|
| **P** - Praise | |
| **R** - Repent | |
| **A** - Ask | |
| **Y** - Yield | |

# Weekly Coach's Prayer Roster

## #CPR

| Player | Spiritual | Education | Family | Athletics |
|--------|-----------|-----------|--------|-----------|
|        |           |           |        |           |
|        |           |           |        |           |
|        |           |           |        |           |
|        |           |           |        |           |
|        |           |           |        |           |
|        |           |           |        |           |
|        |           |           |        |           |
|        |           |           |        |           |
|        |           |           |        |           |
|        |           |           |        |           |

# Day 28 - Fasting

Each week you've been asked, **what is the mountain you're wanting to see moved?** Read back through your playbook looking over the mountains that haven't been moved yet. This week, fast over them. Lay them at the feet of Jesus again. As you fast today, pray over them again and again without ceasing.

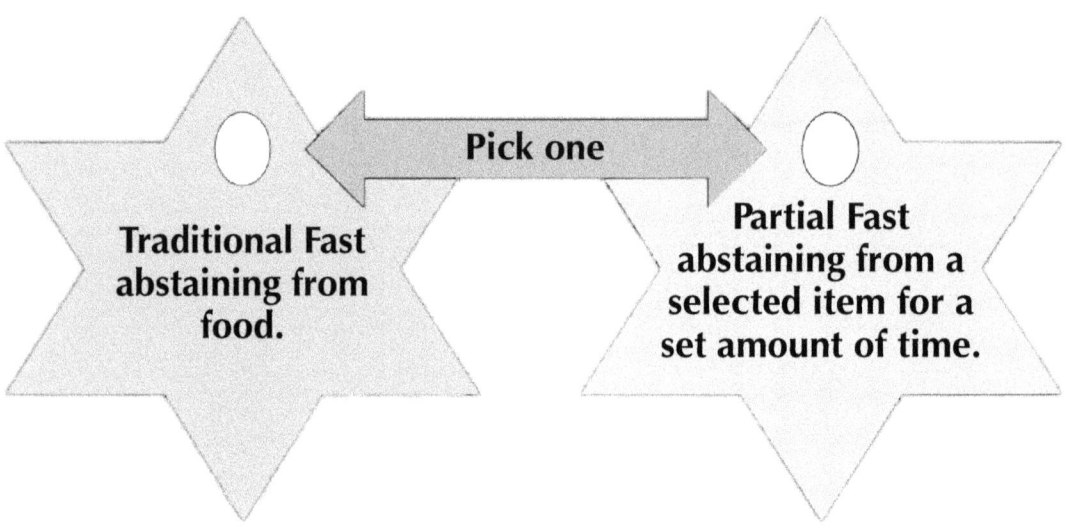

**Pick one**

**Traditional Fast abstaining from food.**

**Partial Fast abstaining from a selected item for a set amount of time.**

This week I'm fasting......

# Day 29 - Reflection / Yield

Today, you're going to write yourself a letter. You have six weeks left in this playbook. How do you want to finish? How are you expecting God to show up and show off? Are you willing to be vulnerable? What is your purpose in coaching?

Dear Vulnerability,

_____

_____

_____

_____

_____

_____

_____

_____

# Day 30 – Proclaiming victories / Surrendering everything

As this week comes to an end, take time to name the victories on and off the field. Go into detail. Take time to praise our heavenly Father with every stroke of the pen.

_____

_____

_____

_____

_____

_____

Was there a mountain you saw moved this week? If so, how is your heart towards it today? If not, what is the mountain you're wanting to see moved? Lay it down again and again at the feet of Jesus.

_____

_____

_____

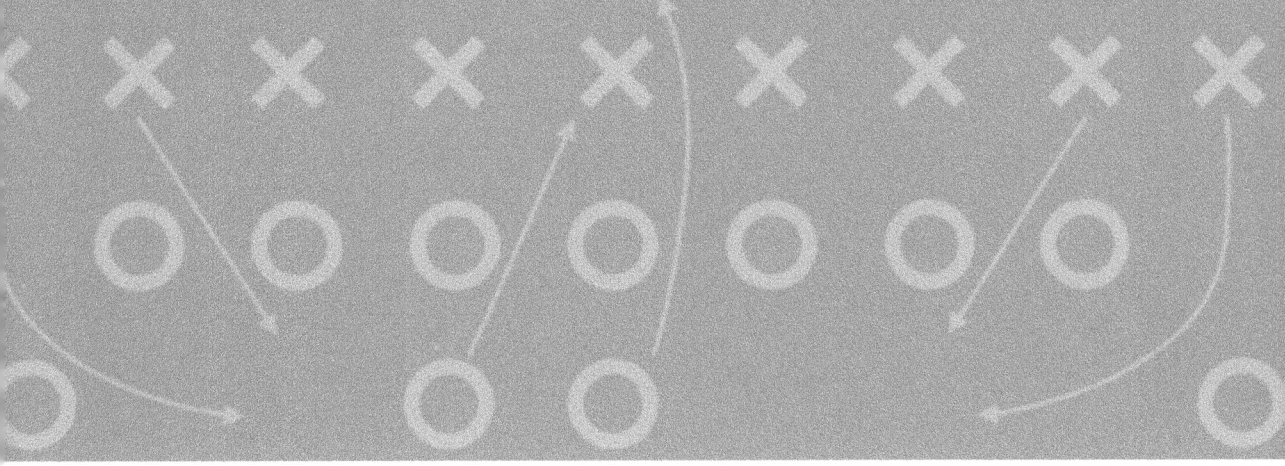

*Jesus answered, "I am the way and the truth and the life.*
*No one comes to the Father except through me."*
*(John 14:6 NIV)*

While leading a team of athletes in the Dominican Republic, we were blessed to partner with their local Fellowship of Christian Athletes team. During our time there, we participated in baseball, softball, and basketball in various forms from clinics to live game play. The days were LONG and HOT!

It was during this time one young man named Tony became very ill from dehydration. He thought he was drinking enough. But what was usually good enough back home wasn't cutting it in the tropical humidity. Through this illness and receiving IV treatment, God brought Tony to his spiritual end. He began to realize that he didn't know Jesus as his Lord and Savior, and he had just been going through the motions of his spiritual walk. God worked on Tony's heart for the rest of that trip, and after we had returned, He kept working on him. We had been back about a week when Tony fully and completely accepted Christ as his Savior, and fully surrendered his life to ministry. He fully grasped God's calling on his life, and it began with Jesus's salvation of his soul.

# Day 31 - Journal

Everything we do starts and ends with Jesus. He is our truth and life. Reading through your prayer roster, build your prayer bracket. If you have a player who doesn't know Jesus as their personal Lord and Savior, add them this week. If you have already had them a week, add them again. Expand your bracket if needed.

Take time to go meet with your players one-on-one for a moment. Ask them how they are doing this week. Is there anything they would like to get off their chest? Let them know you're listening.

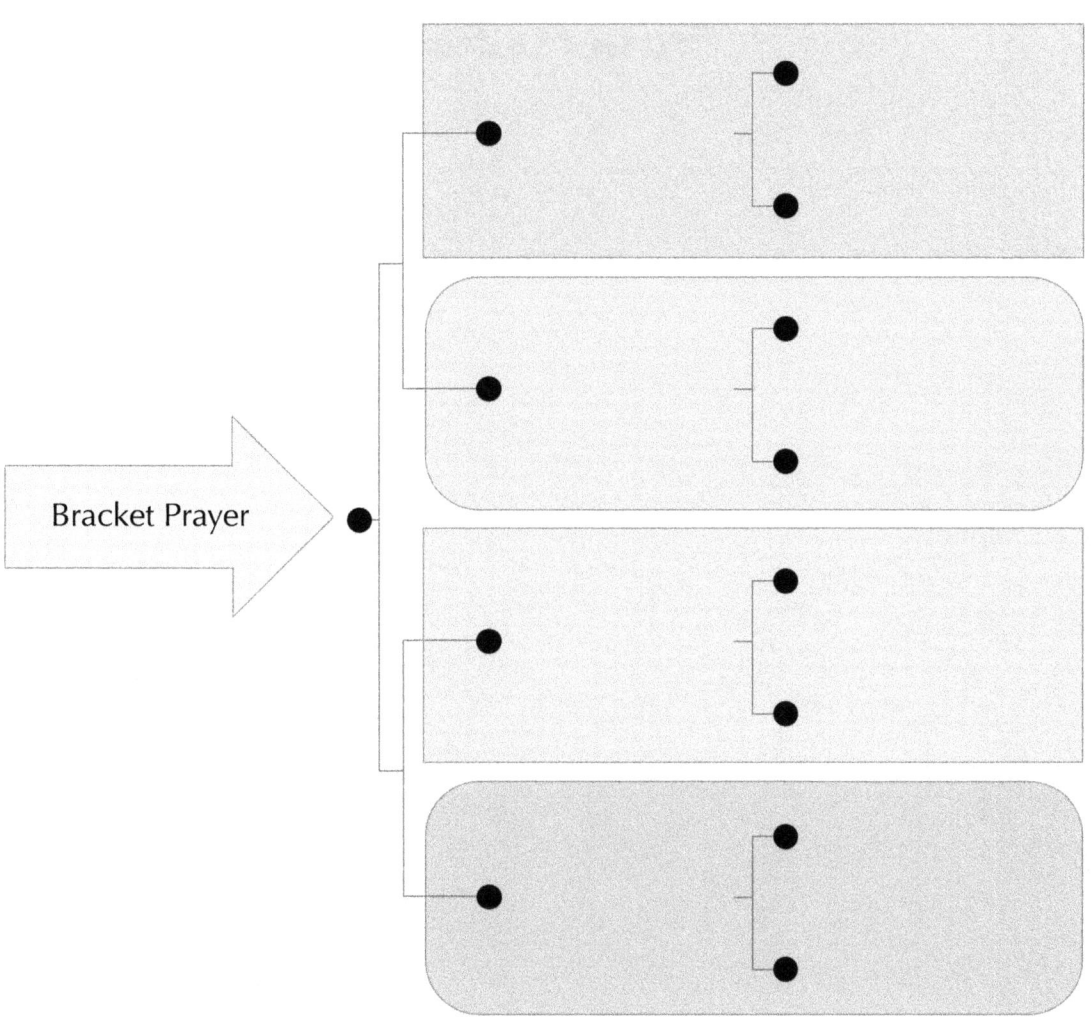

# Day 32 - Prayer Walking

Ask the Holy Spirit, "What are You showing me this week?" Take time to listen as you walk your coaching surface.

| Prayer Chart | |
|---|---|
| **P** - Praise | |
| **R** - Repent | |
| **A** - Ask | |
| **Y** - Yield | |

# Weekly Coach's Prayer Roster

#CPR

| Player | Spiritual | Education | Family | Athletics |
|--------|-----------|-----------|--------|-----------|
|        |           |           |        |           |
|        |           |           |        |           |
|        |           |           |        |           |
|        |           |           |        |           |
|        |           |           |        |           |
|        |           |           |        |           |
|        |           |           |        |           |
|        |           |           |        |           |
|        |           |           |        |           |
|        |           |           |        |           |

# Day 33 - Fasting

Name the players one by one you're fasting for this week. Lay their salvation at the feet of Jesus.

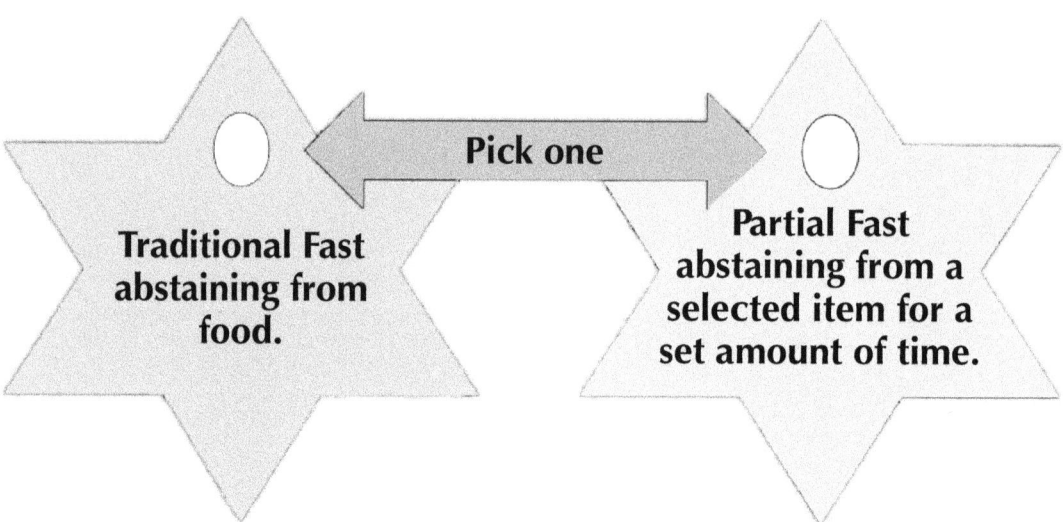

**Pick one**

**Traditional Fast**
abstaining from
food.

**Partial Fast**
abstaining from a
selected item for a
set amount of time.

This week I'm fasting......

# Day 34 - Reflection / Yield

*Jesus answered, "I am the way and the truth and the life.*
*No one comes to the Father except through me."*
*(John 14:6 NIV)*

What are you longing for this week? Is there anything you're lamenting this week?

## Day 35 – Proclaiming victories / Surrendering everything

As this week comes to an end, take time to name the victories on and off the field. Go into detail. Take time to praise our heavenly Father with every stroke of the pen.

_____

_____

_____

_____

_____

_____

_____

Was there a mountain you saw moved this week? If so, how is your heart towards it today? If not, what is the mountain you're wanting to see moved? Lay it down again and again at the feet of Jesus.

_____

_____

_____

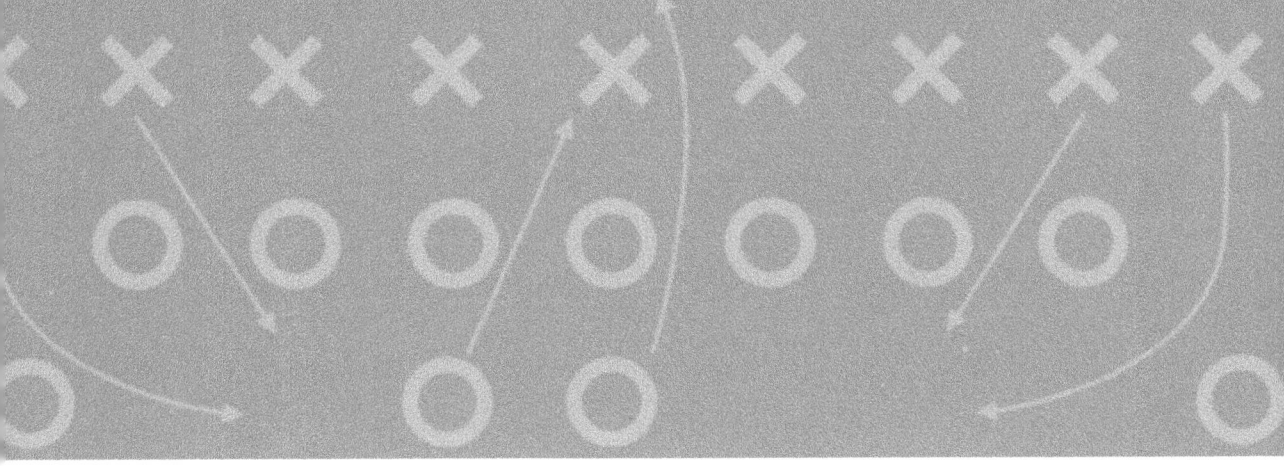

*…while our presentable parts need no special treatment. But God has put the body together, giving greater honor to the parts that lacked it, so that there should be no division in the body, but that its parts should have equal concern for each other. If one part suffers, every part suffers with it; if one part is honored, every part rejoices with it. Now you are the body of Christ, and each one of you is a part of it.*
*(1 Corinthians 12:24–27 NIV)*

It was a triple-digit summer day when the water cooler went dry in the dugout. Up until then, many had not paid attention to who filled it or even made sure it was packed on the bus. It was at that moment everyone was looking around asking whose job it was to fill it back up. I remember a senior walking over and taking it **happily** to refill for the team. Some would say that's not a senior's job, but he saw a need for his team and filled it. Here we see when Paul was writing to the church at Corinth about working in unity as a whole, not one part being greater than another. As your team continues to grow, press into building each one equally in their responsibilities. Mix up the traditions, allowing God an opportunity to show off and build new relationships and traditions.

# Day 36 - Journal

This week, build your prayer bracket from your player roster by mixing up the traditions that set the boundaries so many fall within.

Take time to go meet with your players one-on-one for a moment. Ask them how they are doing this week. Is there anything they would like to get off their chest? Let them know you're listening.

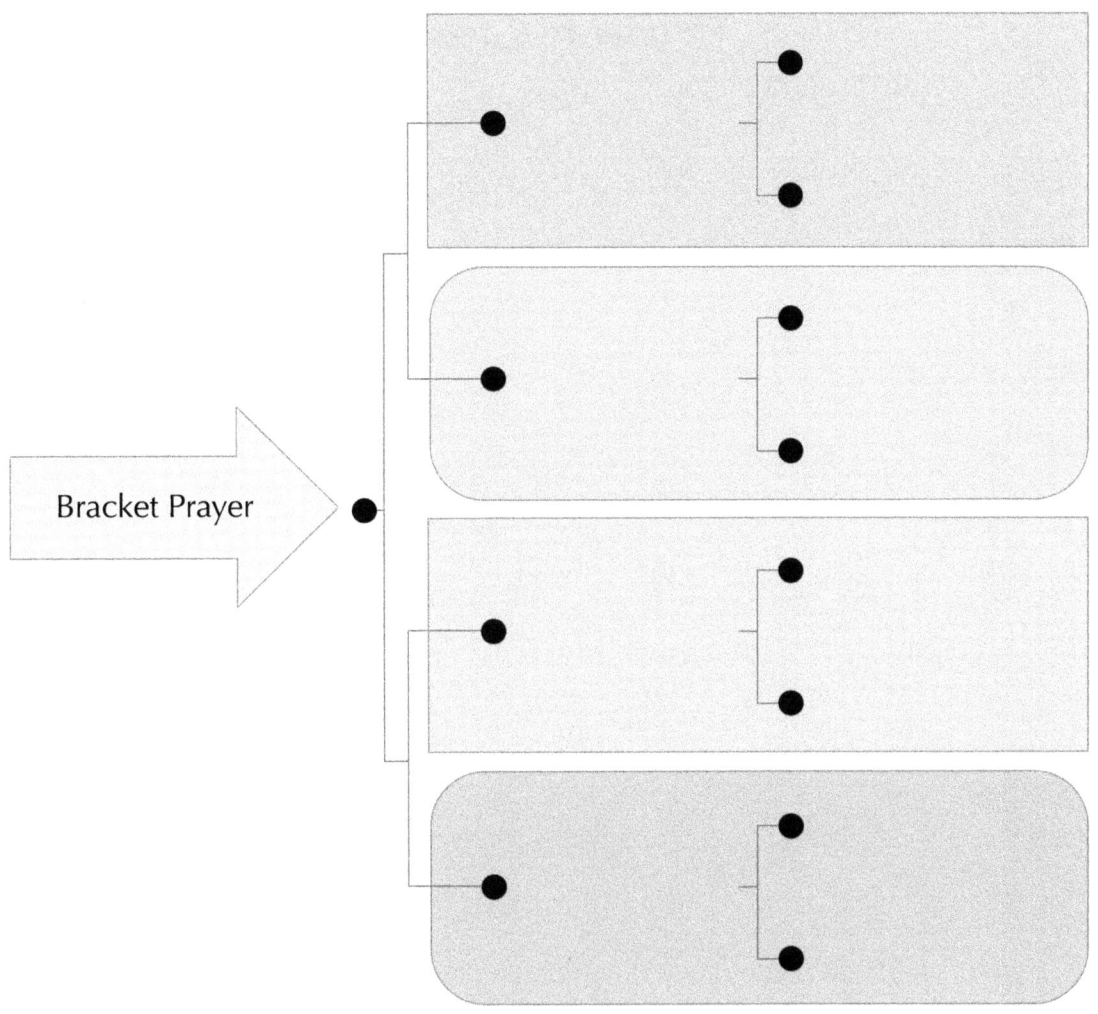

# Day 37- Prayer Walking

As you walk out this day, ask the Holy Spirit, "What are You asking of me this week?" Listen with intent, willing to move your feet where He guides you.

## Prayer Chart

| | |
|---|---|
| **P** - Praise | |
| **R** - Repent | |
| **A** - Ask | |
| **Y** - Yield | |

# Weekly Coach's Prayer Roster

## #CPR

| Player | Spiritual | Education | Family | Athletics |
|--------|-----------|-----------|--------|-----------|
|        |           |           |        |           |
|        |           |           |        |           |
|        |           |           |        |           |
|        |           |           |        |           |
|        |           |           |        |           |
|        |           |           |        |           |
|        |           |           |        |           |
|        |           |           |        |           |
|        |           |           |        |           |
|        |           |           |        |           |

# Day 38 - Fasting

Is there an area that needs to be restructured for your team? Is there an area that you've seen great improvement? Today, fast over the area you're longing to see keep improving or one you know needs to be restructured. Ask the Holy Spirit, "What are You asking of me this week?"

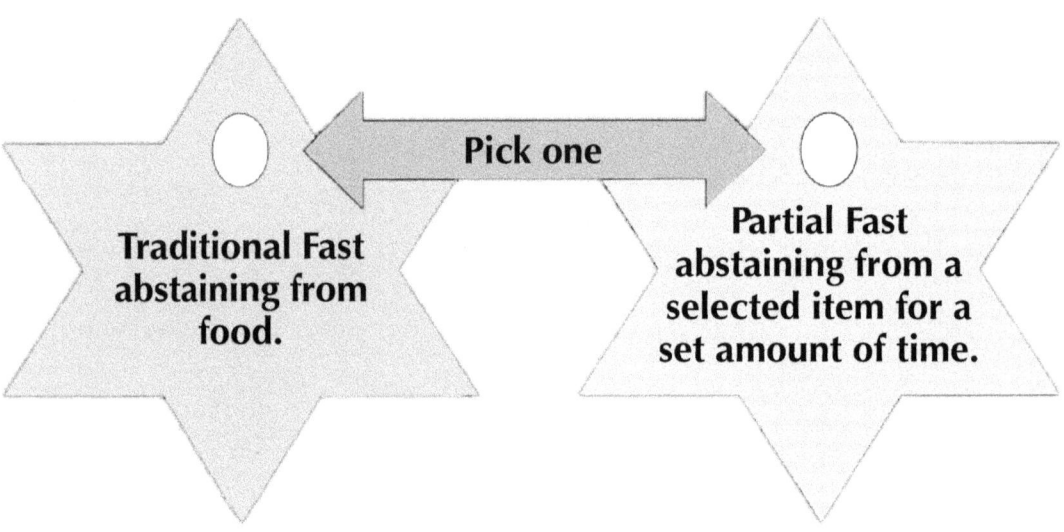

**Pick one**

**Traditional Fast abstaining from food.**

**Partial Fast abstaining from a selected item for a set amount of time.**

This week I'm fasting......

# Day 39 - Reflection / Yield

Today, write yourself a letter about how you want to see change or improvement. Go in detail of the desires of your heart. Take a moment to reflect on this week and where you've felt the Holy Spirit move. Lay it all at the feet of Jesus.

# Day 40 – Proclaiming victories / Surrendering everything

As this week comes to an end, take time to name the victories on and off the field. Go into detail. Take time to praise our heavenly Father with every stroke of the pen.

_____

_____

_____

_____

_____

_____

_____

Was there a mountain you saw moved this week? If so, how is your heart towards it today? If not, what is the mountain you're wanting to see moved? Lay it down again and again at the feet of Jesus.

_____

_____

_____

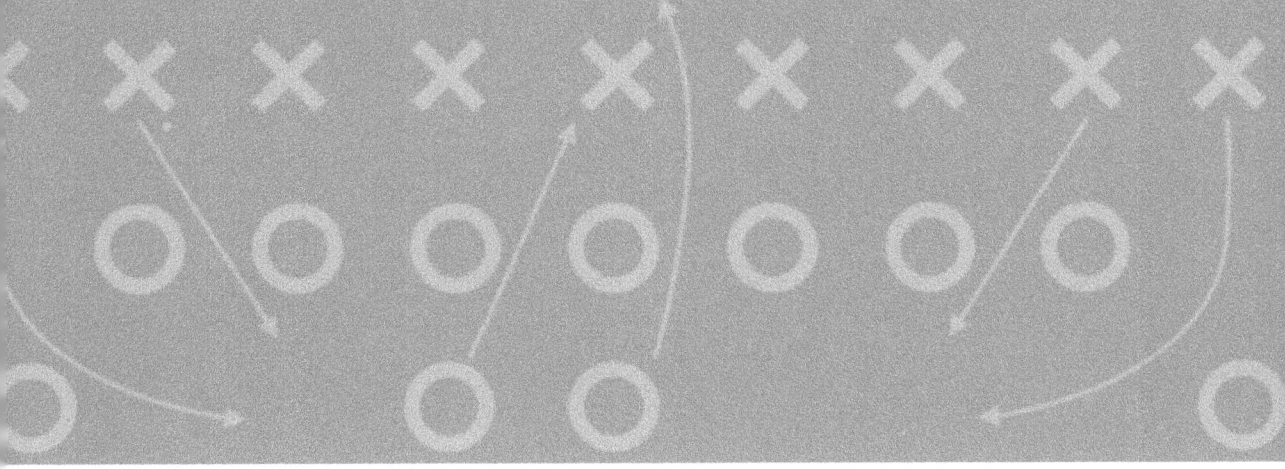

## WEEK 9

*And we are confident that he hears us
whenever we ask for anything that pleases him.
(1 John 5:14 NLT)*

*Lord, You alone, You are the very beginning, the end, and the very
essence of love within me. Open my eyes and heart to see You as
You see and love others through me.* — Heather Hodges

# Day 41 - Journal

Take time building your prayer bracket from your player roster and know Jesus hears every request made unto Him. Ask Him for anything with confidence; He is listening. As you lay your players at His feet this week, know you're pleasing our heavenly Father.

Take time to go meet with your players one-on-one for a moment. Ask them how they are doing this week. Is there anything they would like to get off their chest? Let them know you're listening.

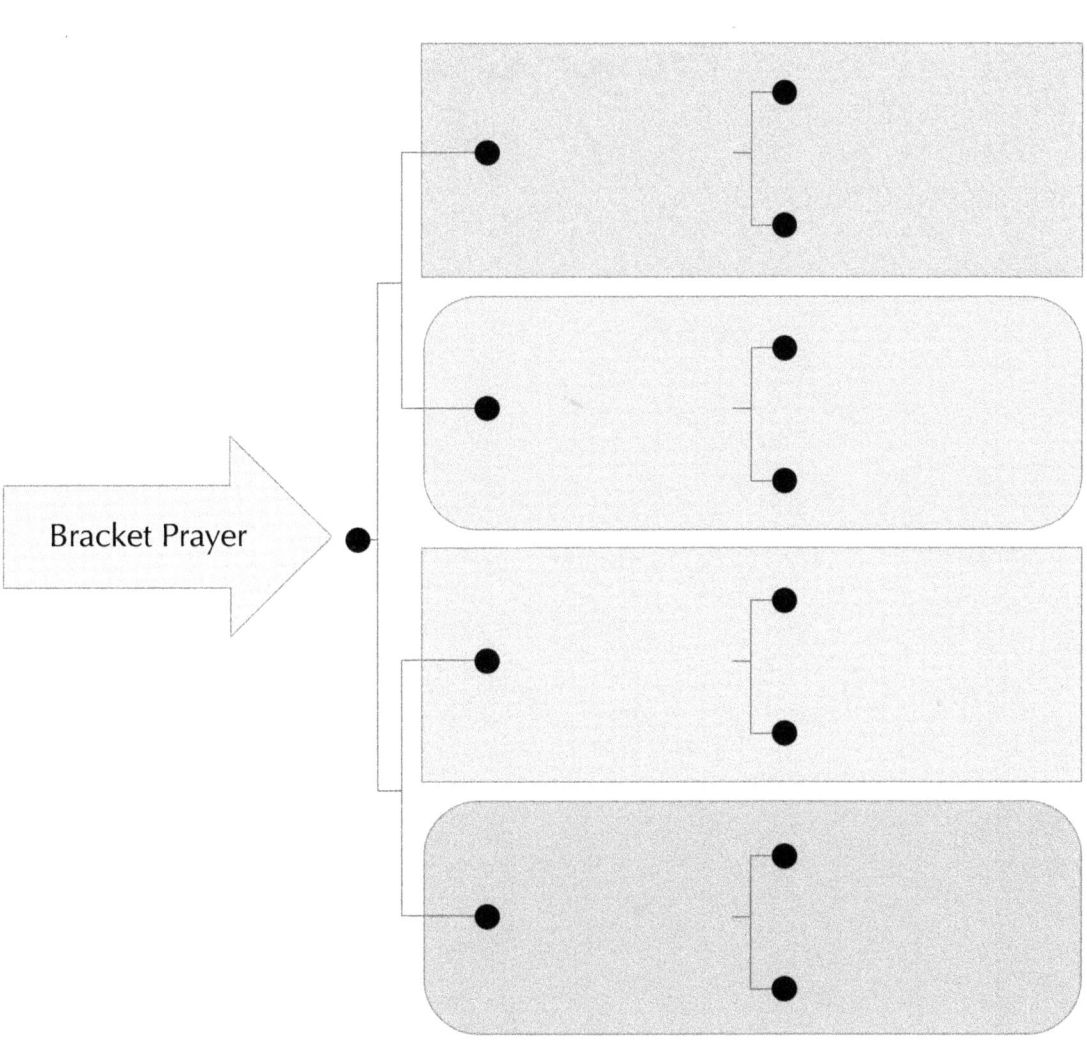

# Day 42 – Prayer Walking

As you prayer walk your coaching surface this week, ask the Holy Spirit, "What are You showing me?" Pray, "Speak to me, Lord, for I am listening."

## Prayer Chart

| | |
|---|---|
| **P** - Praise | |
| **R** - Repent | |
| **A** - Ask | |
| **Y** - Yield | |

# Weekly Coach's Prayer Roster
## #CPR

| Player | Spiritual | Education | Family | Athletics |
|--------|-----------|-----------|--------|-----------|
|        |           |           |        |           |
|        |           |           |        |           |
|        |           |           |        |           |
|        |           |           |        |           |
|        |           |           |        |           |
|        |           |           |        |           |
|        |           |           |        |           |
|        |           |           |        |           |
|        |           |           |        |           |
|        |           |           |        |           |

# Day 43 - Fasting

*Lord, You alone, You are the very beginning, the end, and the very essence of love within me. Open my eyes and heart to see You as You see and love others through me.* – Heather Hodges

Ask the Lord to open your eyes and heart today through your fast. Ask Him to pour out His essence of love within you. As you fast over your team, be willing to move as the Lord guides your heart.

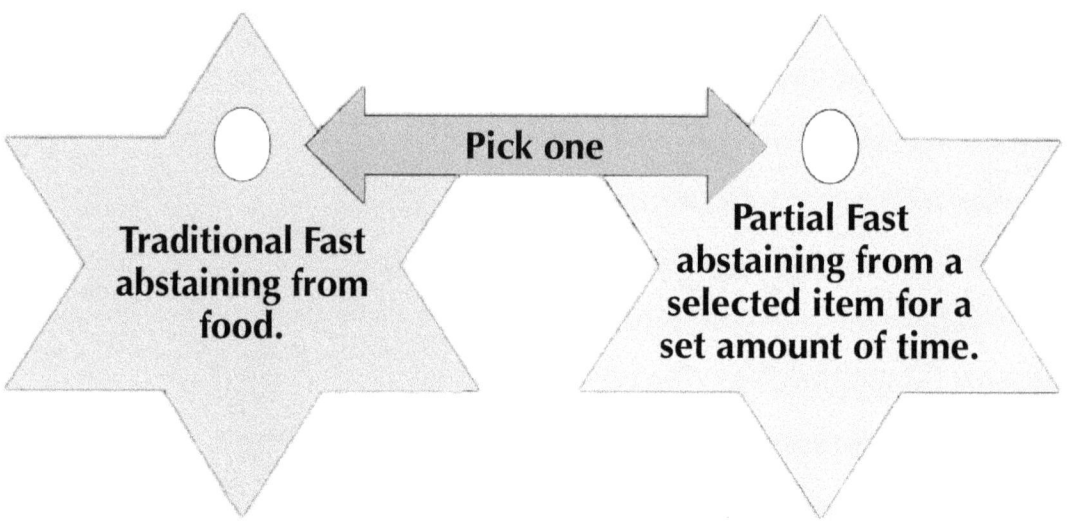

This week I'm fasting......

# Day 44 - Reflection / Yield

What did the Holy Spirit show you this week? Are you willing to walk it out? Is there a certain player that keeps coming to mind? Have you taken time to pray and connect?

By being intentional with every step in coaching, you're giving Jesus full opportunity to move these mountains into the seas. Take time to write out in detail what's on your heart this week. Be honest. Be raw.

_____

_____

_____

_____

_____

_____

_____

_____

_____

# Day 45 – Proclaiming victories / Surrendering everything

As this week comes to an end, take time to name the victories on and off the field. Go into detail. Take time to praise our heavenly Father with every stroke of the pen.

_____

_____

_____

_____

_____

_____

_____

Was there a mountain you saw moved this week? If so, how is your heart towards it today? If not, what is the mountain you're wanting to see moved? Lay it down again and again at the feet of Jesus.

_____

_____

_____

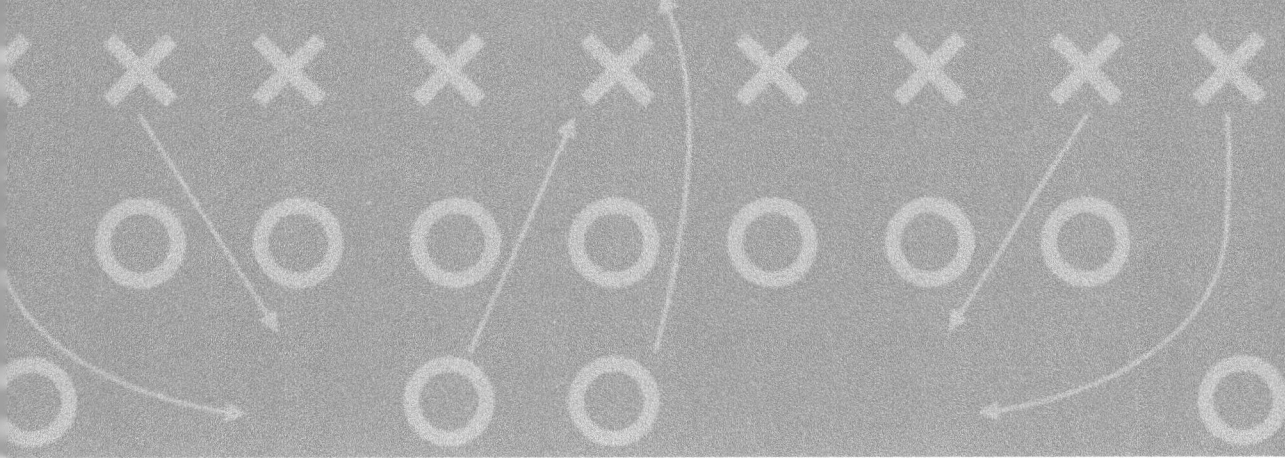

*Do not let any unwholesome talk come out of your mouths, but only what is helpful for building others up according to their needs, that it may benefit those who listen. (Ephesians 4:29 NIV)*

If you've ever played for my husband, you know one of his rules is no cussing on the field. I remember pulling up to practice one day when a young man was very upset in the parking lot. He was ready to quit because he said he couldn't get his mouth under control; the cuss words just kept coming out. He was being truthful; they did. I asked him a simple question, "Do you want to play baseball?" He said, "Yes, I love this game."

I said, "Coach Hodges loves and cares for you more than this game of baseball. He loves baseball, but he loves and cares for you more. He has surrendered his coaching to Jesus. At one time, cussing was a struggle for Coach Hodges also. When he stepped into saying yes to Jesus in coaching, it changed him from the inside out. If you're only trying to stop cussing for Coach, it's not going to work, but when you surrender it to Jesus, that's a game changer." I encouraged the young man to go talk to Coach again and explain how he was trying. He did and that day accepted Jesus as his personal Lord and Savior.

Your players watch and hear everything! It's hard! We're all human and will fail more than once. How we walk beside our players and direct them to Jesus is the game changer. It will require us to be vulnerable by sharing the struggles we've walked through and by pointing them to Jesus alone.

# Day 46 - Journal

Build your prayer bracket from your player roster. Is there an area you need to surrender and allow Jesus full access to this week? If someone only knew Jesus through the words you spoke, who would He be to them?

Take time to go meet with your players one-on-one for a moment. Ask them how are they doing this week. Is there anything they would like to get off their chest? Let them know you're listening.

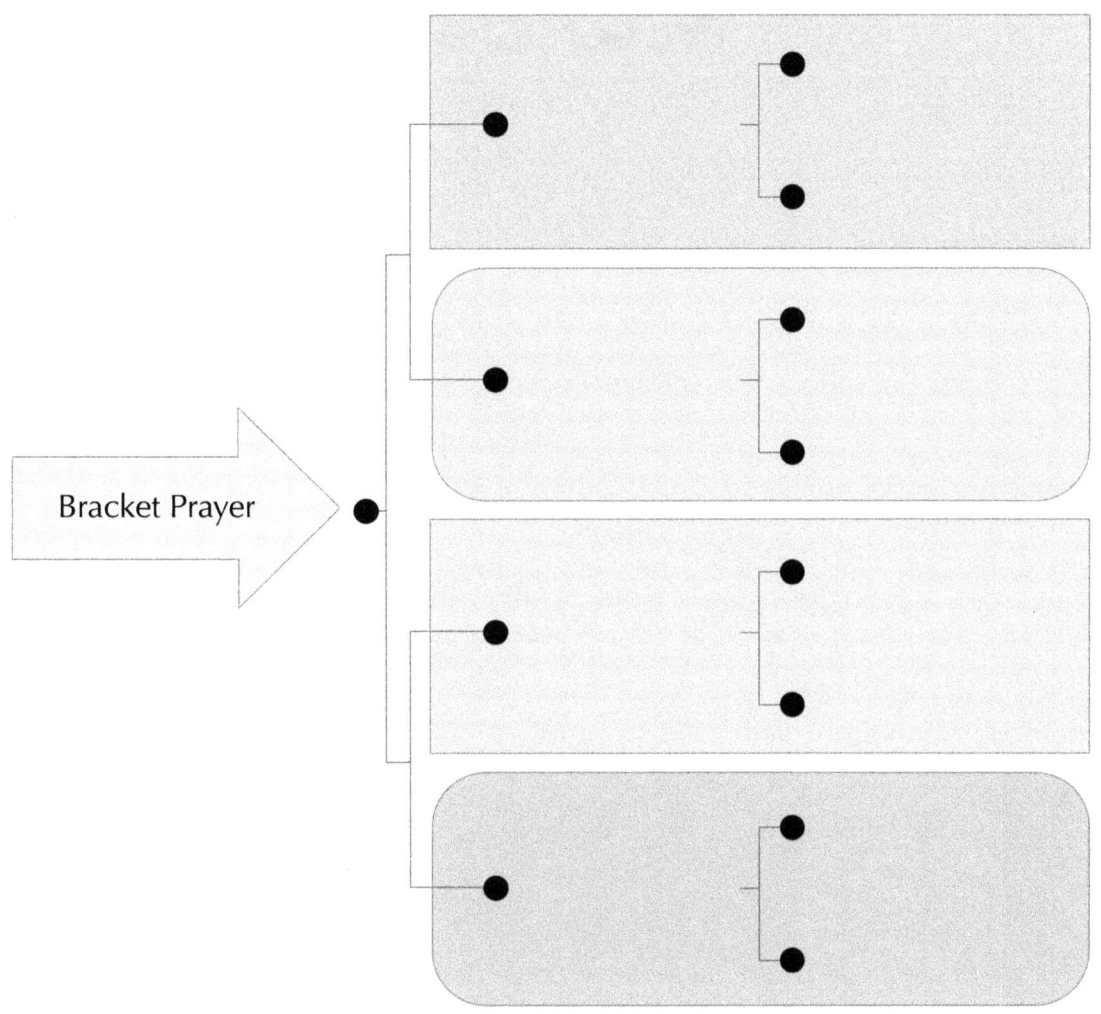

# Day 47 – Prayer Walking

As you prayer walk this week, ask the Holy Spirit, "What are You saying to me?"

## Prayer Chart

| | |
|---|---|
| **P** - Praise | |
| **R** - Repent | |
| **A** - Ask | |
| **Y** - Yield | |

# Weekly Coach's Prayer Roster

#CPR

| Player | Spiritual | Education | Family | Athletics |
|--------|-----------|-----------|--------|-----------|
|        |           |           |        |           |
|        |           |           |        |           |
|        |           |           |        |           |
|        |           |           |        |           |
|        |           |           |        |           |
|        |           |           |        |           |
|        |           |           |        |           |
|        |           |           |        |           |
|        |           |           |        |           |
|        |           |           |        |           |

# Day 48 - Fasting

*Do not let any unwholesome talk come out of your mouths, but only what is helpful for building others up according to their needs, that it may benefit those who listen. (Ephesians 4:29 NIV)*

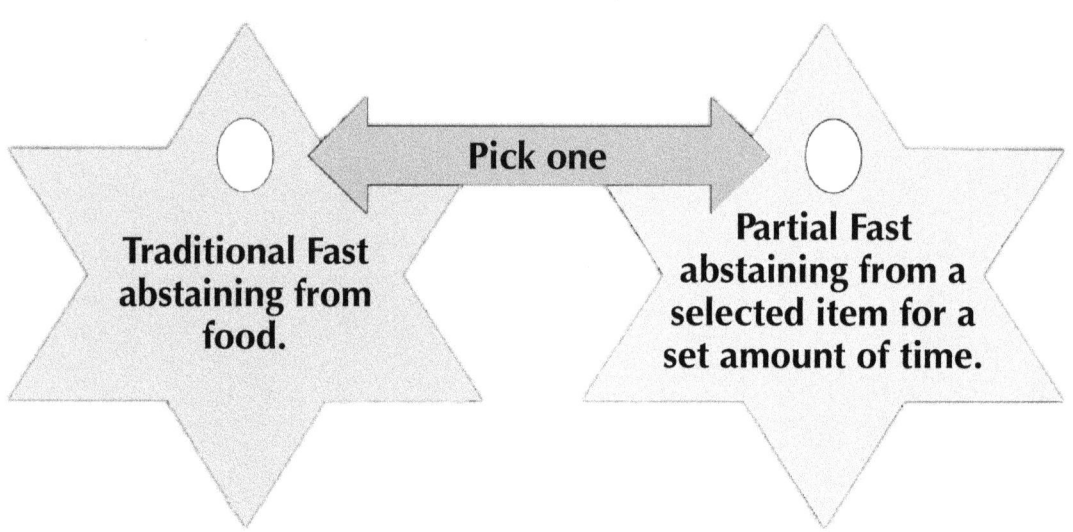

This week I'm fasting......

# Day 49 - Reflection / Yield

What did the Holy Spirit say to you this week? Are you willing to walk it out fully, surrendering it to Jesus? Is there an area you see needing adjusting in your coaching style? Are you willing to adjust?

Take a moment to write out where you are today. Go in detail. (Are you tired of reading "go in detail" yet? God loves when we give Him all the details.) If you find yourself needing to adjust the way you speak, then pray this verse, asking God to help you: "Do not let any unwholesome talk come out of your mouths, but only what is helpful for building others up according to their needs, that it may benefit those who listen" (Eph. 4:29 NIV).

# Day 50 – Proclaiming victories / Surrendering everything

As this week comes to an end, take time to name the victories on and off the field. Go into detail. Take time to praise our heavenly Father with every stroke of the pen.

_____

_____

_____

_____

_____

_____

_____

Was there a mountain you saw moved this week? If so, how is your heart towards it today? If not, what is the mountain you're wanting to see moved? Lay it down again and again at the feet of Jesus.

_____

_____

_____

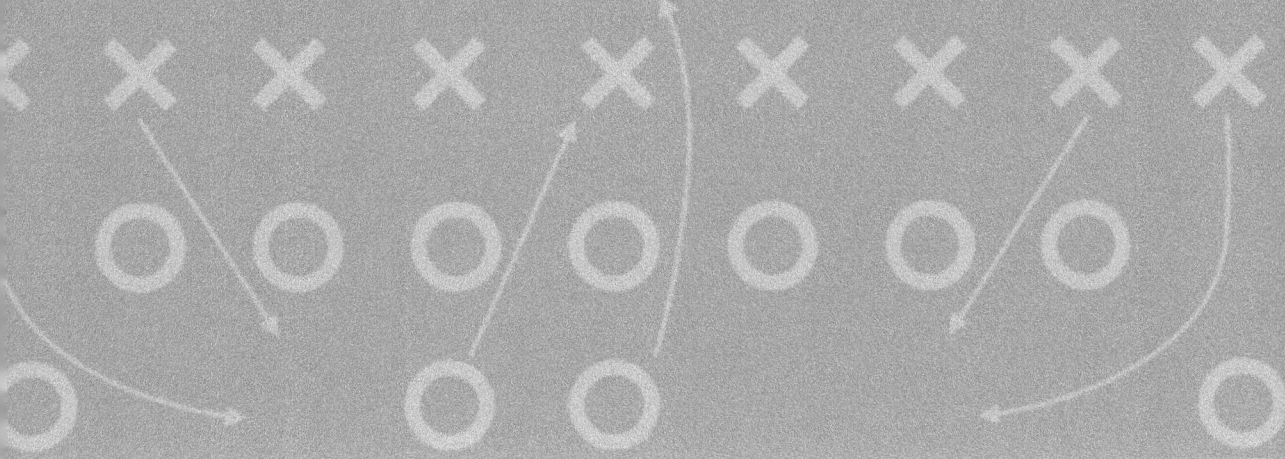

*For the Spirit God gave us does not make us timid,*
*but gives us power, love and self-discipline.*
*(2 Timothy 1:7 NIV)*

Paul wrote this to Timothy during his imprisonment before he was put to death. He identifies Timothy as a fellow missionary, one who is boldly proclaiming the gospel of Jesus Christ. Throughout this playbook, you've had the opportunity to step into being the coach Jesus is calling you to be. This week, pray this verse while holding true to the writer who scribed these words for us while sitting in prison himself. We're given freedoms in greater depths than ever before in the history of our world. Where believers were martyrs in the day of old in their homeland, God has placed you in a land of freedom able to boldly proclaim His name. You have the ability to be a living witness for Christ to every player who will ever call you "Coach." Grab it and run with it!

# Day 51 - Journal

How does having this freedom within your homeland change your approach to sharing Jesus?

Even though you may have a secular job, the ability to live out your faith openly allows others to catch Jesus within you. Remember, people catch your actions as your words can be limited in public entities.

Build your prayer bracket from your player roster, knowing Jesus is going to meet you there. Ask the Holy Spirit, "What are You asking of me?"

Take time to go meet with your players one-on-one for a moment. Ask them how they are doing this week. Is there anything they would like to get off their chest? Let them know you're listening.

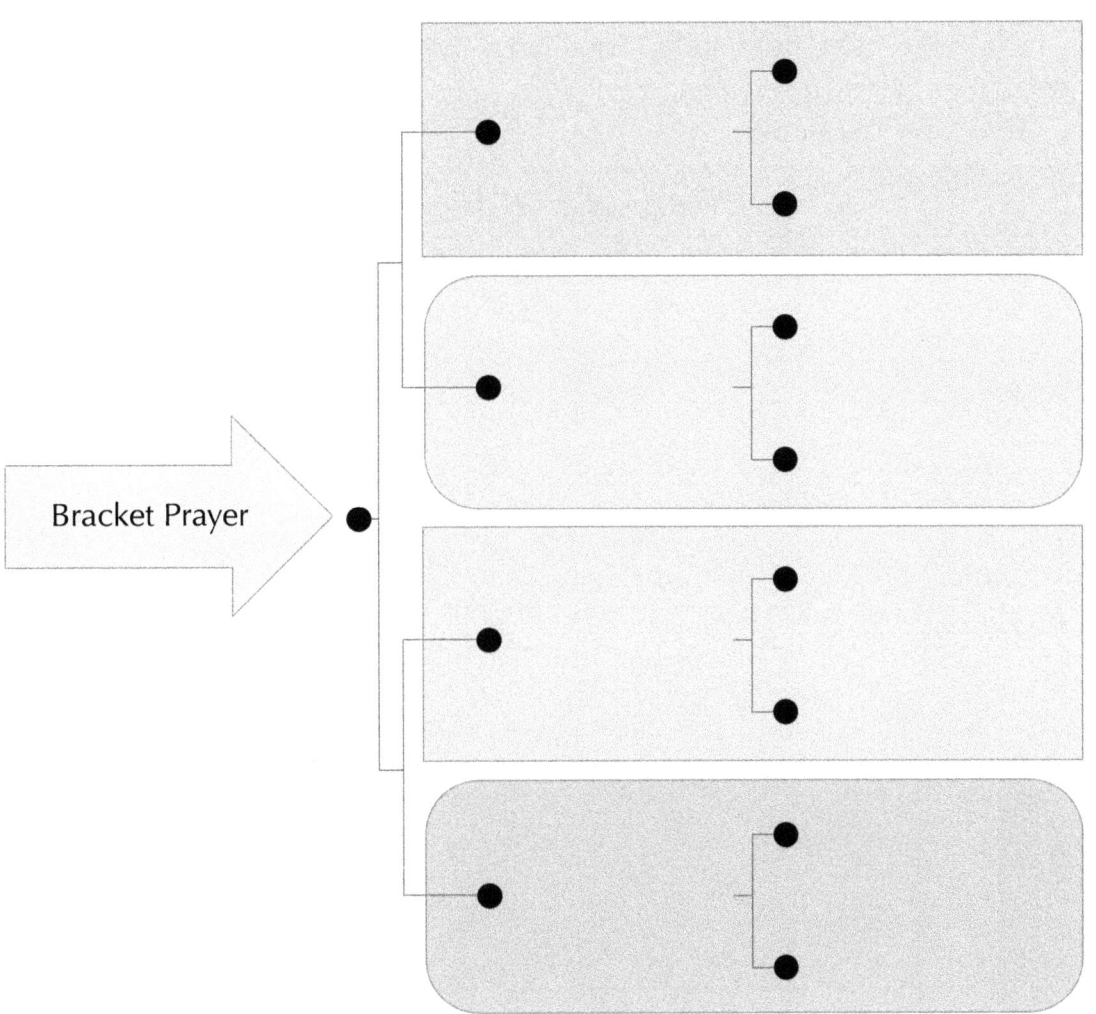

# Day 52 – Prayer Walking

By prayer walking on your surface, you are proclaiming Christ from the intimate space within your heart. Know that every step is a step of obedience outwardly for others to see Jesus.

Pray your roster aloud today. Ask the Holy Spirit, "What are You asking of me?"

Take time to listen.

## Prayer Chart

| | |
|---|---|
| **P** - Praise | |
| **R** - Repent | |
| **A** - Ask | |
| **Y** - Yield | |

# Weekly Coach's Prayer Roster

## #CPR

| Player | Spiritual | Education | Family | Athletics |
|--------|-----------|-----------|--------|-----------|
|        |           |           |        |           |
|        |           |           |        |           |
|        |           |           |        |           |
|        |           |           |        |           |
|        |           |           |        |           |
|        |           |           |        |           |
|        |           |           |        |           |
|        |           |           |        |           |
|        |           |           |        |           |
|        |           |           |        |           |

# Day 53 - Fasting

You have the ability to be a living witness for Jesus to every player who will ever call you "Coach." This week, fast over your coaching field once again. Ask God to show you anything He wills to show you this week.

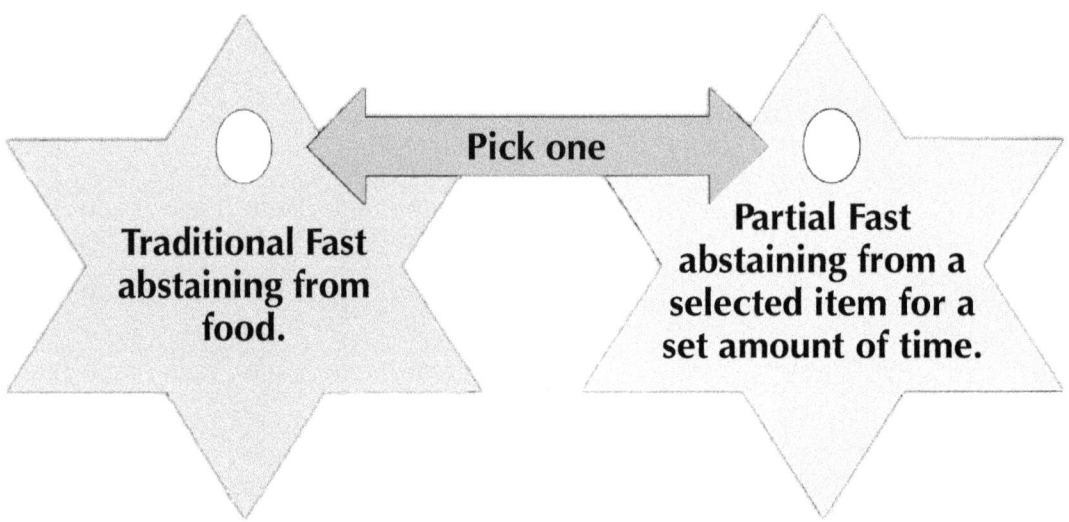

This week I'm fasting......

# Day 54 – Reflection / Yield

*For the Spirit God gave us does not make us timid,*
*but gives us power, love and self-discipline.*
*(2 Timothy 1:7 NIV)*

How does this verse land on your heart knowing that the spirit the Lord gives us does not make us timid, but gives us power, love, and self-discipline?

Take a moment to reflect back over this week. What did the Holy Spirit ask of you?

_____

_____

_____

_____

_____

_____

_____

_____

## Day 55 – Proclaiming victories / Surrendering everything

As this week comes to an end, take time to name the victories on and off the field. Go into detail. Take time to praise our heavenly Father with every stroke of the pen.

_____

_____

_____

_____

_____

_____

_____

Was there a mountain you saw moved this week? If so, how is your heart towards it today? If not, what is the mountain you're wanting to see moved? Lay it down again and again at the feet of Jesus.

_____

_____

_____

# POSTSEASON REFLECTIONS

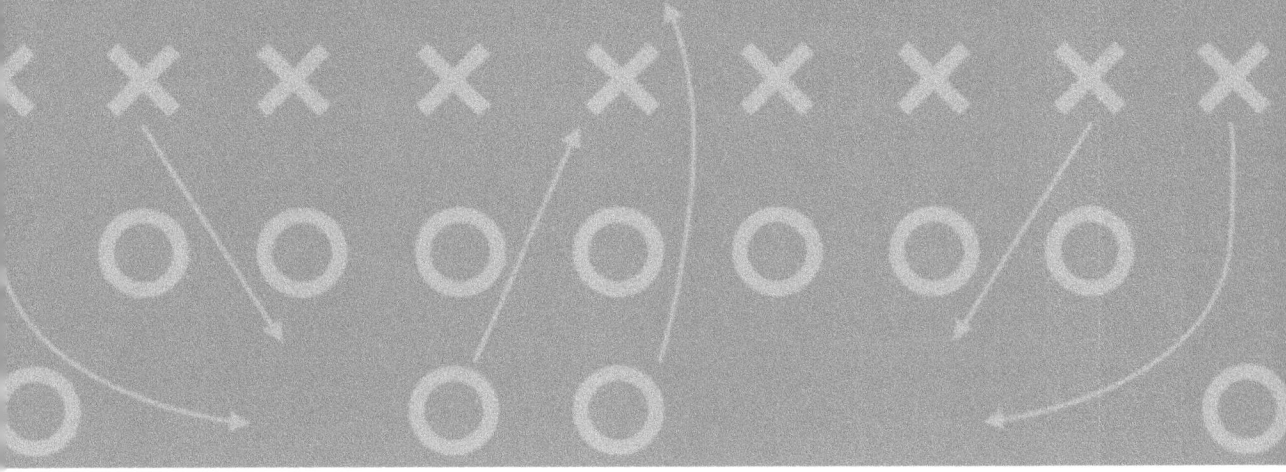

*For I was hungry and you gave me something to eat,*
*I was thirsty and you gave me something to drink,*
*I was a stranger and you invited me in…*
*(Matthew 25:35 NIV)*

It was the last FCA huddle of the year when I heard the sweet whispers of God bring these verses to me. As tears poured down my face, all I could do was raise my hands in worship in the quietness of the cafeteria. In coaching, we pray for the salvation of every single player that crosses our path. We pray, asking our heavenly Father to make Himself known in abundance to our players, not for an abundance of earthly possessions, but of His love, mercy, grace, knowledge, and His purpose for their lives. How God had a plan for them before they were even born.

This year, God did answer our prayers. We had a player who turned his life around. This kid didn't have the best of the best. Sometimes he wasn't sure where he would rest his head at night or if a hot meal was always going to be an option. He showed me so much in the little things. He always showed up, he was always willing to help clean up afterwards, he was a friend to my boys, and he had a half smile most days. Every week after FCA, he would hang back to take the extra food.

That week was different. That week hit a little deeper. That week, he was no longer on this side of heaven to take the food home. He was home with Jesus; Jesus had prepared a table for him with lots and lots of room. We laid him to rest that morning with a gym full of friends and family, days before he was supposed to walk across that very stage in graduation.

It was then in the quietness of the cafeteria God whispered these words: "For I was hungry and you did give Me something to eat; I was thirsty and you did give Me something to drink; I was a stranger and you did take Me in." In our time of grief and regret, wishing we had done more, God gave us comfort in this reminder that we did what we could. In God's sovereignty, he knew the day this young man would be in heaven.

You may never see the victory of a state championship in this career. You may never have the victory column larger than the losses, or perhaps you will. One thing is certain—the eternal victories will never be reset and there will be a day each of us will pass away from this earth.

Coming to the end of *Coaching with a Purpose*, I want to encourage you to take time for deep reflections. Look back over the past sixty days and ask God to speak to you through the Holy Spirit, to help you have an open heart to see all the movements that have taken place. Praying the eternal victories brings tears of joy knowing that heaven is potentially growing from your walk of obedience.

## To Do List:

- Highlight the wins you've seen.
- Circle the prayers that you're still laying at Jesus's feet.
- Walk in the assurance of knowing every prayer lifted has been heard.
- Go back and read the letter you wrote yourself in Week 6.

Allow yourself time to soak in all you've walked through.
How would you sum up the past sixty days?

*Lord, You alone, You are the very beginning, the end, and the very essence of love within me. Open my eyes and heart to see You as You see and love others through me.* — Heather Hodges

# CHARTS YOU CAN COPY

# Weekly Coach's Prayer Roster

### #CPR

| Player | Spiritual | Education | Family | Athletics |
|--------|-----------|-----------|--------|-----------|
|  |  |  |  |  |
|  |  |  |  |  |
|  |  |  |  |  |
|  |  |  |  |  |
|  |  |  |  |  |
|  |  |  |  |  |
|  |  |  |  |  |
|  |  |  |  |  |
|  |  |  |  |  |
|  |  |  |  |  |

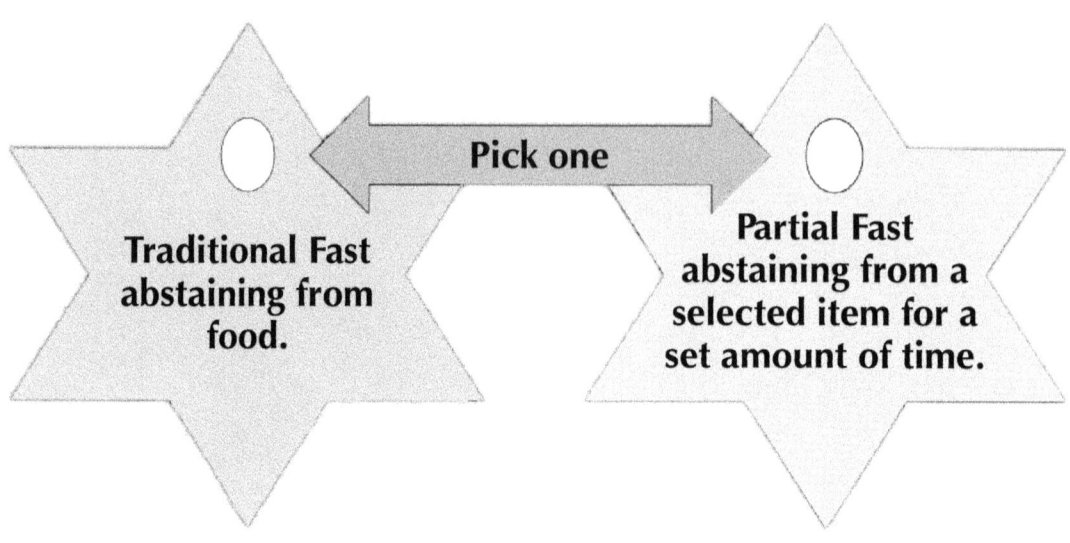

This week I'm fasting......

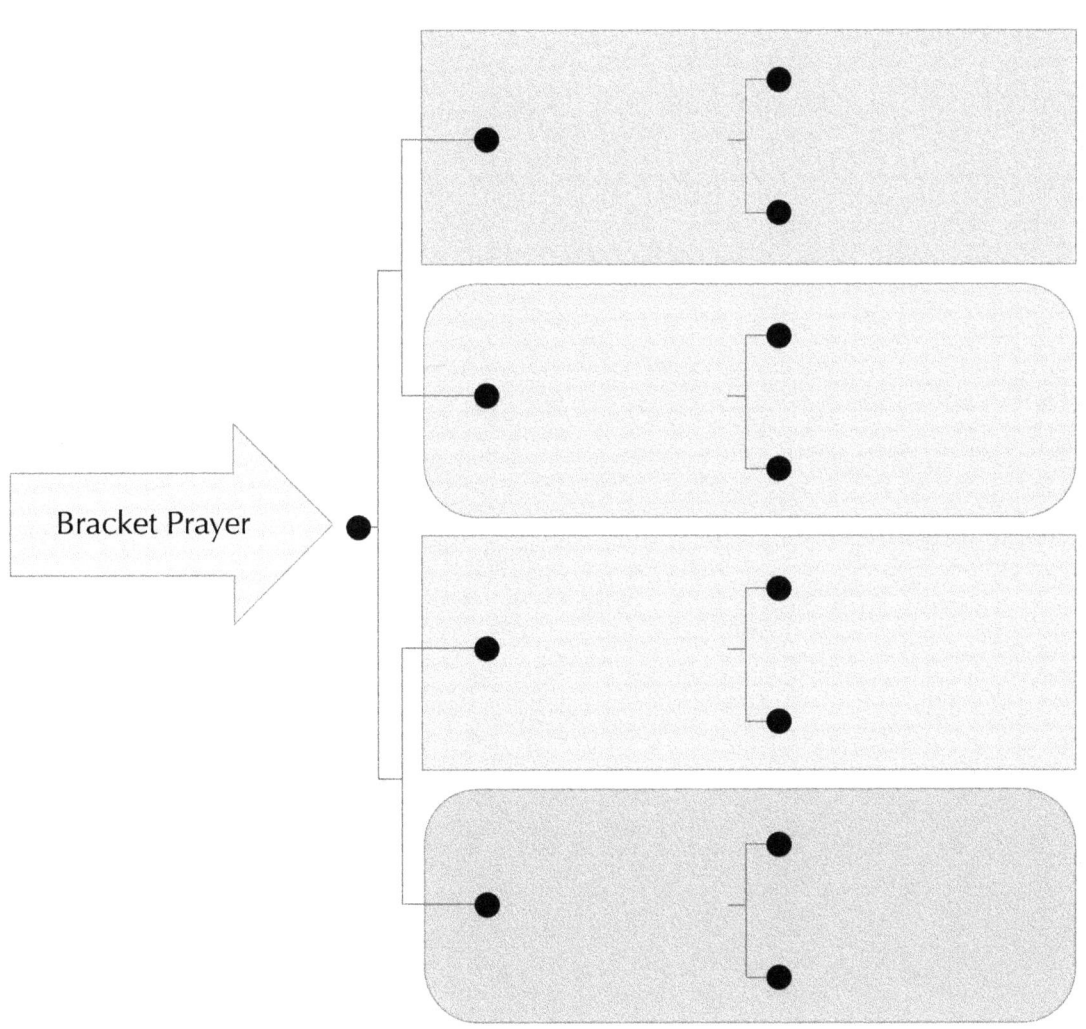

Bracket Prayer

www.ingramcontent.com/pod-product-compliance
Lightning Source LLC
Chambersburg PA
CBHW041144120626
46547CB00020B/3096